WHAT IS THE WELFARE STATE FOR?

The status quo is broken. The world is grappling with a web of challenges that could threaten our very existence. If we believe in a better world, now is the time to question the purpose behind our actions and those taken in our name.

Enter the What Is It For? series – a bold exploration of the core elements shaping our world, from religion and free speech to animal rights and war. This series cuts through the noise to reveal the true impact of these topics, what they really do and why they matter.

Ditching the usual heated debates and polarizations, this series offers fresh, forward-thinking insights. Leading experts present groundbreaking ideas and point to ways forward for real change, urging us to envision a brighter future.

Each book dives into the history and function of its subject, uncovering its role in society and, crucially, how it can be better.

Series editor: George Miller

Visit **bristoluniversitypress.co.uk/what-is-it-for** to find out more about the series.

Available now

Forthcoming

PAUL SPICKER is a writer and commentator on social policy. His published work includes 22 books, several reports and shorter works and nearly a hundred academic papers. His studies of housing and welfare rights developed from his early career; since then, his research has included studies related to benefit delivery systems, the care of old people, psychiatric patients, housing management and local antipoverty strategy. He is a consultant on social welfare in practice, and has done work for a range of agencies at local, national and international levels. After teaching at Nottingham Trent University and the University of Dundee, he held the Grampian Chair of Public Policy at Robert Gordon University from 2001 to 2015. He is now an Emeritus Professor of Robert Gordon University.

A selection of Paul Spicker's published work is available on open access at **https://tinyurl.com/69f5vvsa** or at **https://observant-paulspicker.wordpress.com/**.

WHAT IS
THE WELFARE STATE
FOR?

PAUL SPICKER

Ⓑ

First published in Great Britain in 2025 by

Bristol University Press
University of Bristol
1–9 Old Park Hill
Bristol
BS2 8BB
UK
t: +44 (0)117 374 6645
e: bup-info@bristol.ac.uk

Details of international sales and distribution partners are available at
bristoluniversitypress.co.uk

British Library Cataloguing in Publication Data
A catalogue record for this book is available from the British Library

ISBN 978-1-5292-5075-6 paperback
ISBN 978-1-5292-5076-3 ePub
ISBN 978-1-5292-5077-0 ePdf

Cover design: Tom Appshaw

Bristol University Press' authorised representative in the European
Union is: Easy Access System Europe, Mustamäe tee 50, 10621
Tallinn, Estonia, Email: gpsr.requests@easproject.com

CONTENTS

1

WHAT IS A WELFARE STATE?

Around the world, something extraordinary has been happening. The 'welfare state' has long been thought of as the province of rich western economies, and the term is used most to refer to those countries which have made the most generous provision for their citizens. Discussions of the 'welfare state' in those countries have often been critical of, and sometimes hostile to, the idea that people need the support of welfare services or cash benefits. In the UK and USA, any discussion of the 'welfare state' is likely to be taken as a question of attacking or defending what's there.

If we shift the focus to developing countries, however, governments are looking at the issues quite differently. In the course of the last 25 to 30 years, there has been an explosion of interest and activity in the field of social welfare. This is most evident in middle-income and emerging economies, but it has gone some way beyond that. The few countries which do not provide social services and social protection are now the exception, rather than the norm. Governments have been coming to accept that social welfare provision is something they are expected to do, no less than economic or foreign policy.

The 'welfare state' generates a good deal of passion, but there is very little agreement about what one actually is. There is a small battalion of scholars out there who try to analyse these movements by monitoring and quantifying the activity of different countries. This is not straightforward: many welfare states, especially those in Europe, have welfare services provided by institutions that are not part of government. There are many actors and many objectives. If we want to understand what welfare states are doing, the idea of a consistent 'welfare regime' is a poor description of what actually happens. Welfare states can have many objectives – for example, providing a safety net, offering security, redistribution, developing social rights and supporting the economy. When we dig down deeper into the role of different social services, such as health care or social security, the picture becomes more complex still. Most contemporary systems are put together with several aims in mind, and will apply different criteria both within and between services.

The way to make sense of all this is not to crunch numbers. The biggest numbers, such as how much money gets spent on health care or pensions, mainly reflect a position where some countries have more to spend than others. That does not do very much to help us understand why so many governments, of all political colours, are developing this sort of policy. Examining the history of welfare states leads in another direction entirely, mainly helping to explain the differences between welfare states rather than their common elements. This book focuses, instead, on what 'welfare states' are supposed to do – quite literally, what the welfare state is for.

Welfare states matter. They are about the difference that governments, welfare services and social institutions make to people's lives. But the idea of the welfare state is not just a description of what governments do. It is a moral concept – helping us to see what ought to be done. This is a direction of movement, not a destination. That direction has been leading towards the progressive extension of services and the inclusion of growing numbers of people.

Some of the justifications for welfare are moral; some are practical, such as helping the economy. Some serve the political interests of rulers. The provision of welfare is an important route to legitimacy, and it is used in both democratic countries and authoritarian regimes to meet that end. The pressure to develop welfare systems further has proved to be irresistible. Conventional criticisms of the welfare state, from right and left, have largely failed to get to grips with the main issues posed by the growth of such systems – issues such as coping with a mass role, finding the resources, or organizing service delivery (which has to depend on the kind of service being considered – some services are delivered in person, some are not). In the pages that follow, I want to discuss what has been happening and what the challenges are.

The state and social welfare

There are three common ways of understanding what a welfare state is. The first takes it to be all about the provision of social services by the state: government provides a range of benefits and welfare services for its population. We can find references to 'welfare states' in countries around the world; they seem to have little in common apart from the fact that the government does something about providing services. American sources, for example, trace the 'welfare state' in the USA to the Social Security Act of 1935,[1] when the engagement of the US federal government was very limited. That Act mainly provided for insurance-based protection for old age and some forms of industrial disability. If that very low bar is the threshold, most countries in the world have now passed it.

The range of services that states provide is not clear-cut, but some broad generalizations are possible. Begin with health care and access to medicine. Universal, free and comprehensive health care, of the kind found in the UK, is unusual, but most developed countries will commonly make provision for care in hospitals, and for public health (such as provision for vaccinations). When it comes to primary care, or other forms of care that people can receive without being admitted to hospital, the picture is more mixed, but many states that do not provide those services directly have made general provision for financial support or health insurance. The widest gaps in provision tend to fall in a third category, that of medical goods – pharmaceuticals, aids and treatments – where the level of support is often partial. However, we should not focus too firmly on developed countries. Just about every country in the world spends some proportion of its national income on health services. In theory, this now serves about five-sixths of the world's population; in practice, because service delivery is difficult, it probably applies to about 60%.[2]

The other most common form of provision is education, especially education in schools – education is possibly the only field of welfare activity where a collective experience (being part of a school class), rather than an individual one, is treated as the norm. Around the world, there has been a substantial expansion of state-sponsored elementary education – some countries (such as Uganda, Ethiopia, Kenya and Malawi) have tried to do this all at once with a 'big bang', with mixed success.[3] Provision may be patchy, but over 80% of all children globally, and nearly 60% of children in the least developed countries, now complete an elementary education.[4]

Third, there are cash benefits. In the course of the last 25 years or so, there has been a deluge of new, large-scale national schemes. More than half the world's population is covered by at least one social protection scheme, and the vast majority of countries – more than 180 – now have legislative programmes covering old age, disability and sickness.[5] There is a bewildering variety of provision in the global South, depending on the contingencies that are to be met, arrangements for access, state ownership, coverage and relative generosity.[6]

The largest element of such schemes is provision for older people, now available to more than three-quarters of the world's population. The coverage of other issues, particularly unemployment, is more limited, and there may well be failures of coverage in practice.[7] The COVID-19 pandemic made it even more difficult to remedy that: in recent years, the emphasis has shifted to more selective, 'targeted' programmes, and there have been cuts in public spending, but the schemes seem to have survived despite their relatively recent foundation. A report for the International Labour Organization comments that

> the world is currently on two very different and divergent social protection trajectories: high-income countries (85.9 per cent) are edging closer to enjoying universal coverage; and upper-middle-income countries (71.2 per cent) and lower-middle-income countries (32.4 per cent) are making large strides in closing protection gaps. At the same time, low-income countries' coverage rates (9.7 per cent) have hardly increased since 2015.[8]

There is still some way to go, then. But part of the message to draw from this is that governments around the world are trying to do something, even if that something is not good enough yet. Social security benefits have become part of a government's role.

Health, education and social protection are not the whole story. There was a time when the provision of housing would routinely have been considered in an account of the welfare states. William Robson, a professor of public administration, suggested in the 1970s that 'Public housing is so important a part of national policy that one could almost determine the claim of a country to be a welfare state by the magnitude of its effort in this sphere ...'.[9] That comment was defensible fifty years ago, because housing was a major part of provision in the most developed economies; but it is so far removed from current ways of thinking that it might well strike present-day readers as odd. In discussions of the welfare state, the provision of housing and support for housing has faded from view. That shift is difficult to explain, because housing is basic to well-being. It is a major element of individual welfare in its own right; it is central to people's participation in society; and it is hard to avoid having at least a fixed address as a precondition for the delivery of other services. States in the developed world may have provided housing directly, in the form of 'public housing'; they may have given financial support for 'social housing'; they may have specialized services to help people who are homeless; and they may legitimately see the operation of developers and landlords as part of their field of interest in social policy. None of those is certain, however, and when international comparisons are being made of 'welfare regimes', the role of housing policy is likely to be left out of the consideration.

Beyond these four pillars, the picture of government engagement with social welfare provision becomes much more fragmentary. The label of the 'personal social services' has been taken to cover social work, 'social care' and child protection. Social care, mainly support for older people and those with disabilities, includes both support at home and residential services; child protection will include responding to neglect or abuse, fostering and adoption, and residential care for children. These services may be typical of welfare states, and certainly their absence would count as a deficiency – the precarious existence of street children in developing countries is evidence of a lack of services. However, these services are not generally thought of as defining welfare states – partly, one suspects, because they are rather more difficult to codify and compare than expenditure on health or cash benefits.

Many governments make, or have made, a major contribution to the social fabric: libraries, roads, streetlights, water supplies, postal services, communications, policing, sewers, surface drainage, energy supplies, public space and so forth. Because so much of this was done before governments even realized that 'welfare states' were possible, they might not be considered as part of the pattern of services that governments have a duty to secure and maintain in a welfare state. Nevertheless, they are clearly an expression of the same principle: that states have the responsibility to make people's lives better.

Most comparisons of welfare states rely on a stripped-down account of conventional services, leaving out lots of other important issues in the hope that their selections at least point in the right direction. A recent paper by two German authors suggests that there is 'an uncontested semantic core', consisting of 'old-age security, health insurance, poverty relief, work-accident insurance, labour legislation and unemployment insurance, and sometimes even extends to a number of other policy areas, such as housing and education'.[10] So labour legislation makes the cut, but public health doesn't? I've explained about housing, but why is education only considered 'sometimes'? What about other long-established services, such as family benefits, the care of prisoners or employment services? The more closely one looks at the laid table, the less settled it seems to be. Does a welfare state have a minimum wage? What does a welfare state do about domestic violence? How about fostering and adoption? Is street-lighting part of the profile? Do welfare states do things about climate change that other states do not? It is difficult to see any clear relationship between the general idea of the welfare state and the specific services it might provide.

Nevertheless, there is a simple point to draw out of this short review of activities. There is nothing extraordinary about governments providing services that benefit their people. Nearly all the countries of the world do something to provide forms of welfare for their populations, or (more accurately) for some part of their populations. States in the global South are often driven by constraints that are rather different from the developed economies. They are likely to have limited resources, inadequate numbers of trained staff such as doctors, and patchy information (such as a record of who has been born and who has died). Many have partial coverage, working to local criteria when it comes to informal employment, urban or rural living, or responding to the situation of families. It remains true, despite the limitations, that every country does something about health care, almost every country provides some education for their populations, and social protection in the form of cash benefits has become normal. As the historian David Garland comments, 'a welfare state of some description is a vital part of any modern nation'.[11] This is what governments – even bad governments – do.

Welfare systems

The second main concept of the welfare state is not really about the 'state' as such. An emphasis on the role of government is baked into the idea that the welfare state is a 'state', but focussing too narrowly on the state fails to reflect what is really happening. Governments are not necessarily the sole, or even the main, providers of welfare services. The role has been taken by a range of non-government actors, including, among others, voluntary organizations, trades unions, mutual insurers, religious bodies, occupational providers and co-operatives. This has been called 'welfare pluralism'.

The definition of the 'voluntary' sector is ambiguous, because the term 'voluntary' is sometimes taken to encompass any independent, non-profit-making activity: a 'voluntary' hospital, in the USA, may well have public wards, private wards and private beds, and some charitable purposes. One feature of the voluntary sector is the influence of charitable and non-profit services; historically, this is strongly linked to religious organizations, such as churches and waqfs. This in turn is linked to unpaid voluntary work – for example, in fundraising, the membership of boards or the delivery of social services such as food banks. The range is wider than any overview can easily convey; the voluntary sector in the UK has been called 'a loose and baggy monster'.[12]

'Occupational' welfare also covers a range of issues – arrangements that employers make for issues such as social protection (such as occupational health care), pensions, housing (the provision of accommodation) and education (such as apprenticeships). The relationship is primarily contractual, and some occupational benefits are mandated by states as a condition of employment, but it has been extended in some places to cover circumstances that go somewhat further. In France, unemployment benefits are financed and delivered through Unédic, a 'convention' of employers and trades unions.

Mutual aid tends to be overlooked in much of the literature, or treated as a sub-set of the voluntary sector, but it has been hugely important in the development of economic and social institutions – an 'enormous army'.[13] The origins of health services, social insurance and housing societies often lie in mutual aid, a tradition stretching back at least to the guilds of the middle ages.[14] Several states, such as the Nordic countries, built their systems on the basis of mutual aid. Israel's system began with the trades unions; France has a system of mutual insurers (the *mutuelles*) which offer people supplementary insurance, beyond what government offers, and the terms are so beneficial that most people become members.

A range of non-governmental actors can be identified in almost every country, and that acts as an important qualification about the potential role of government in the process. In poorer countries, the delivery of welfare and the management of the economy are likely to be reliant on international organizations or 'civil society' – that is, non-governmental organizations. The management of plural sectors and multiple actors has become a core task for governments. Governments have to adapt what they do to the circumstances. They may like to think that they are in charge, but they may not have the capacity to control what is happening.

A similar reservation might be made about some fully developed 'welfare states', where arrangements have been made to accommodate the influence of 'social partners' – religious institutions, charities, trades unions and employers. Whatever governments choose to do, it is not going to be the whole story. In practice, the process of negotiating, bargaining and developing 'partnership' has become a major part of the management of welfare – not just in countries where the sectors are highly developed, but in every circumstance where the government wishes to exert some influence over the pattern of provision, and 'every circumstance' comes pretty close to saying 'everywhere'.

The welfare state as an ideal type

The third main approach to understanding the 'welfare state' takes a somewhat different approach to specifying what a welfare state is. This is the representation of the welfare state as an 'ideal type': a template to which reality can be compared, to a greater or lesser degree. Many social scientists would agree with John Veit-Wilson that we need to have a 'discriminating definition' of the welfare state, something that separates it from states that are not welfare states.[15] That leads us to the idea that somehow, somewhere, there must be an agreed catalogue of activities that define a welfare state. Some historical accounts begin with the British welfare state, but the model is somewhat older; it can be traced back to the cities of the Low Countries at the time of the Reformation. The review of the system of relief in the city of Ypres, published in 1531 – that is not a misprint – is one of the best documented from that time (that was because the burghers of Ypres needed to give an account that would satisfy the religious authorities, to protect themselves from the charge of heresy). Ypres had schools for both sexes, cash assistance, employment training, residential care, a take-up campaign to persuade people to claim services – and, believe it or not, free medical care for the poor.[16] If that does not count as a welfare state, what does?

Much of the focus of the literature about welfare states has fallen on the richer nations, particularly those that are members of the Organisation for Economic Co-operation and Development. The most influential classification of this kind was developed by Gøsta

Esping-Andersen. His approach is concerned mainly with the balance between state provision and private markets. He identifies 'liberal' welfare regimes, that try to implement measures using commercial markets; 'corporatist' states, that build on a complex network of social institutions to deliver welfare; and 'social democratic' states, that offer state-based welfare outside the scope of the market.[17] But the field is full of countries that fit the ideal only in some respect, and other countries – 'black swans'[18] – do not seem to fit the pattern at all. Commentators and social scientists have responded to the problems by proposing yet more ideal types – among them, the Southern European Model,[19] the Rudimentary model,[20] and even the 'Slightly Universal Rudimentary Welfare Regime'.[21] There are so many divisions and sub-divisions, cutting across a range of services, that it is difficult to know where to draw the lines.

Classifying welfare regimes offers a way of sketching out some different approaches to welfare, but this approach is not much help in understanding what is going on around the world. The empirical evidence is heavily dependent on information from the richest countries. Even within this narrow sample, the diversity of provision and conflicting criteria have confounded many attempts to offer meaningful generalizations – even the best results yield only a partial identification of distinct patterns of provision.[22] The temptation to go fishing for patterns in the data is hard to resist, and if the data from any awkward policy area – such as housing – does not conform with the pattern, it is likely to be dropped from the analysis, yielding results that are much tidier. When this sort of analysis is extended to the development of welfare systems in middle- and lower-income countries, the analysis becomes even more unmanageable. Social scientists have tried to arrive at classifications by crunching the data with a computer, producing 'clusters' of states in different forms of development.[23] The best evidence tends to focus on how much a country spends on different elements of provision, and the realization that poorer countries have less to spend than richer ones does not say very much about their emergent systems – if we want to understand how systems differ, we need to look at the pattern of provision, not its size.[24] Ultimately the broad categorization of regimes is rather too crude to be useful.

The problems run deeper. In the first place, there is no primary unifying principle that applies to every service that a state or a welfare system delivers. No state, anywhere, does everything one way; what is true for some people, and some services, will not necessarily be true for others in the same country. We cannot tell, from knowing generally how any one regime will react to unemployment or housing policy, what it will make of the position of women, or people with disabilities, or migrants – or indeed anything else. Different countries do different things in relation to disability, maternity, higher education, child care or public infrastructure. The position becomes still more complex once it is understood that welfare is provided through many different institutional systems.

It is hardly possible to generalize from, say, the role of local authorities in providing residential care, to the provision of occupational health care by employers, or the place of religious organizations in adoption services. There are multiple actors, following their own lights. Governments may well find that they are only one of many actors within a complex network of provision.

Second, the tests that are being applied seem to have a very limited relationship to policy. We cannot tell, from the information that a welfare state is 'liberal' or 'social democratic', whether or not (for example) social assistance will be tied in with social work, whether cash assistance will be conditional on active job seeking, or what will be done about long-term care.[25] And, third, the classifications are usually based on selective and somewhat limited empirical criteria, such as how much is being spent, rather than how extensive the provision is, who is covered, or what effect it has on redistribution. As more and more relevant factors are taken into account, the classifications become so complex as to be useless. This seems to be a fundamental weakness in the use of ideal types. They simply cannot be expected to take into account all the relevant factors.

There are no criteria we can call on to distinguish the countries we call 'welfare states' from those we don't. The demand for a 'discriminating definition' is a forlorn hope: there are far too many factors that have to be taken into account. All the fields of activity I have been discussing are important in their own right, and it would not be wild to argue that states that do more in these areas are better states than those which do less. Selecting a relatively small number of specific criteria must unavoidably leave out some things that matter a great deal; and, as the number of possible tests expands, the influence of specific factors, even major factors such as gender or disability, is liable to be dwarfed by the combined effect of everything else.

The welfare state as a set of moral principles

These are the three most common ways of looking at the welfare state: the provision of social services by the state, a system of social provision, or an ideal model. Beyond them, I think I can make out a fourth concept. The welfare state can be seen as a set of principles guiding action. This understanding of the welfare state takes it some way away from the kind of empirical social science that has come to dominate comparative social policy analysis. The 'welfare state' is more than a label. It carries with it a set of norms and expectations – telling us what governments *ought* to do, rather than *how much* they do.

This way of understanding the welfare state owes a great deal to the development of services in Britain. When the British welfare state was founded in the 1940s, it was supposed to offer a different kind of service from what had gone before it – even if, as happened very widely, that meant that the welfare state took over the buildings, the officials and some of the rules that had been part of the previous regime. The Elizabethan Poor Laws had existed, in different forms, for 350 years – 1598 to 1948. They offered poor relief on harsh, demeaning terms, intended to ensure that people would avoid it. After the reforms of 1834, the condition of the pauper had to be 'less eligible' – that is, less to be chosen – than the position of the independent labourer. (Many UK politicians still talk as if that was the right test to use.) The British welfare state was supposed, by contrast, to offer services and benefits without the stigmatizing, penal treatment that had been the hallmark of the Poor Laws.

The description of this transition as the foundation of a 'welfare state' was, Garland argues, only developed retrospectively, in the years after the main measures – including the abolition of the Poor Law – had been enacted.[26] The ideas it represents are, nevertheless, powerful. The historian Asa Briggs explained what set Britain's welfare state apart in these terms:

> First by guaranteeing individuals and families a minimum income irrespective of the market value of their work, or their property. Second by narrowing the extent of insecurity by enabling individuals and families to meet certain 'social contingencies' (for example sickness, old age and unemployment) which lead otherwise to individual or family crisis, and third, by ensuring that all citizens without distinction of status or class are offered the best standards available in relation to a certain agreed range of social services.[27]

The first of these conditions identifies the welfare state strongly with the distribution of cash benefits. The second focuses on a specific set of circumstances that might be seen as individual and personal, but which applied to a large number of people. (It is perhaps worth noting that, at the time of the foundation of the British welfare state, this did not seem to apply either to disability or to child care – these were the subject of later developments.) The third condition reinforces this, with a reference to a 'certain agreed range of social services' – though it is striking that Briggs does not treat the content of that range to be central, except for his reference to a minimum income.

There is something else in Briggs' summary that sets the welfare state apart: the argument that the welfare state should be for everyone, that there should be no distinctions on the basis of class or status, and that people should be offered the best possible standards, not just a minimum. The precise constellation of services and contingencies is rather less important, then, than the statement of principle. Services were going to be delivered to people equally, as of right. Richard Titmuss, a leading thinker about social policy, was no fan of the idea of the 'welfare state', but he put it this way:

> One fundamental historical reason for the adoption of this principle was the aim of making services available and accessible to the whole population in such ways as would not involve users in any humiliating loss of status, dignity or self-respect. There should be no shame of inferiority, pauperism, shame or stigma in the use of a publicly provided service: no attribution that one was being or was becoming a 'public burden'. Hence the

> emphasis on the social rights of all citizens to use or not
> to use as responsible people the services made available
> by the community in respect of certain needs which the
> private market and the family were unable or unwilling to
> provide universally.[28]

If the 'welfare state' has defied the efforts of the bean-counters, it is not least because it is concerned with intangibles. Issues such as rights, dignity and self-respect are hard to measure, to test, or to compare, but they, no less than public spending, buildings or facilities, are the sort of things that make for a welfare state.

It is difficult to understand the literature on the welfare state without having some sense of the strength of feeling that comes with it. Social scientists, writers and commentators are not just concerned with describing what welfare states do: they are just as much concerned with questions about what welfare states *should* do. These comments are illustrative: they come from the USA, Belgium, Germany and the UK.

> The welfare state should, wherever possible, improve the
> living conditions of the most vulnerable in society as a
> matter of priority.[29]

> The welfare state should create a system of universal
> benefits and grants that covers a magnitude of risks to
> human wellbeing.[30]

> The welfare state should guarantee a life in freedom, justice
> and solidarity for all people in Germany.[31]

> The role of the welfare state should never be merely to provide financial support, as important as that will always be, but to help people overcome whatever barriers they might face to living an independent, fulfilling life.[32]

This should give us some clue as to what sort of thing we ought to be looking for when we try to make sense of 'welfare states'. The precepts which underpin the welfare state might be identified in the first place with the 'right to welfare' – that people should have a set of general rights, which guarantee them a range of services when specific circumstances arise.[33] Esping-Andersen calls this 'the core idea of a welfare state'.[34] There are reservations to make about the idea, which I will come back to, but for present purposes the idea of a right to welfare says something directly about the aspirations associated with a welfare state: to treat people as equals, to provide for them and protect them.

The second guiding principle is inclusion: the welfare state is always seeking to meet unmet needs, bringing in people who are marginal or excluded. The diversity of provision through different systems adds to that purpose, rather than detracting from it.

The third element is to aim higher: not just to make things a little better, but to provide high quality services rather than a bare minimum. It is open to discussion whether a welfare state has to do more specifically for prisoners' rights, personal care services or action on climate change, but there is a bias towards decency.

2
WHAT HAS GOVERNMENT GOT TO DO WITH IT?

'Government' is a broad term, covering both those who make decisions about law and policy, and those who implement them. The 'state' is broader still, encompassing a set of institutions that develop and implement public policy. Government has conventionally been seen as comprising three main branches: legislative, executive and judicial. The legislative branch sets the laws; the executive branch implements law and government policy; the judicial branch regulates the conduct of government and adjudicates disputes. There is almost never a clear and clean separation of powers. Governments are expected to make policy, to implement it, and to supervise the delivery of services; executive agencies routinely contribute to policy making and to adjudication.

Many books about political theory have not moved on from the model of the 'power state' that once dominated the way that people understood the role of government. Government, in this account, is seen first and foremost as a way of exercising compulsion. The sociologist Max Weber defined the state as 'a human community that (successfully) claims the monopoly of the legitimate use of physical force within a given territory.'[1] This definition is widely cited, but it is plainly wrong: governments do not claim a monopoly of force. To take the most obvious example, the American constitution explicitly reserves the right to use force to the population at large – that is why Americans have the right to bear arms. Less obviously, many states have been quite prepared to accept a hefty degree of interpersonal force in other circumstances, such as domestic violence against women or the corporal punishment of children. The most that can be said is that governments use physical force as well. Governments can make people do some things, such as military service or sending children to school; and they can use this power to protect some people from other people, for example through policing and the exercise of criminal law.

Governments and states have a range of other powers and capabilities. They make laws – not just criminal laws, but laws governing contracts, family relationships, property ownership, trade and much else besides. The laws regulate the behaviour of people and organizations towards each other; in principle, they also regulate their own behaviour. However, compulsion is far from being the only, or even the main, way that governments can act. Most governments have a range of economic powers. They use them, not just to steer the economy, but to pay for things they want to happen; they can mount events, employ people, or more generally they can use those powers to change economic behaviour, offering subsidies and incentives. Governments can provide services directly, or buy them from independent providers. Then, beyond all this, they have a range of 'soft' powers: they can bargain, negotiate, plan, declare policies and priorities, persuade or encourage activity. One striking development in the course of the last thirty years has been the widespread adoption of public strategy documents and social action plans, a development encouraged and sometimes required by international organizations such as the World Bank, the International Monetary Fund and the European Union.[2] It has become a routine part of how many governments work.

Using their powers in combination, governments have been able to take a wide range of actions which add up to a social policy. If they want to achieve minimum standards, they can both impose restrictions and subsidize higher standards. If governments want to provide services which might otherwise not be available, such as schools or medical care, they can purchase facilities, employ staff, provide financial support to patients and establish social rights. Using housing policy to eliminate slums is another common example, involving compulsory demolition, regulation of building and financial support for alternative provision.

We might perhaps ask: what happens when governments don't take on these tasks? The question may seem removed from reality, but it has often turned out that way. It was true of much of Europe in the 18th and 19th centuries, when governments were trying to restrict their engagement to an absolute minimum. In the absence of government provision, what emerges doesn't look much like the sort of market found in economics textbooks, because commercial markets don't function well when people have no money. Some people will have their needs unmet; some will depend on charity and the support of religious organizations; and many, sometimes most, will turn to mutual aid. Left to their own devices, without support, people band together to offer each other solidarity – not a woolly sentiment, but a practical acknowledgement of mutual responsibility – and social protection.[3] In many welfare states, governments came late to the party, and have had to make choices about the extent to which they would work with established networks, complement them or take on their roles.

Social policy

The welfare state is usually taken to fall into the area of 'social policy', but social policy stretches across three broad areas of public policy. The first of these is economic policy. Every modern government, pretty much without exception, treats the management of the economy as part of its responsibilities. That will be interpreted in different ways, of course, but the idea that this is something that governments do is generally accepted. It was not generally accepted in the

19th century, when 'laissez-faire' or non-intervention was supposed to be norm; but that was also a time when states were routinely engaging in attempts to encourage economic development.

The second main aspect of social policy is found in policies for society. Most governments have such policies, intended either to reflect social norms, such as the place of 'the family', or to establish the norms that governments believe they should encourage. Among the many examples there are laws covering birth, sexuality and marriage. Laws governing participation in the labour market probably have more to do with social priorities than they do with economic ones.

Third, there are social welfare services. Such services are fundamental to any concept of the welfare state, and the role of government in their provision has become more prominent as time has gone on. Governments do not have to make the provision directly: they can buy the social welfare services, they can sub-contract, they can create financial incentives for providers, and they can create other agencies and institutions to do it.

What these three areas have in common is a commitment to welfare – a belief that it is up to the government to do things and to create the conditions that will make people's lives better. The very first use of the term 'welfare state' in English – actually a translation of the German word, *Wohlfahrtstaat* – defined it as 'The idea that the State should not merely protect the persons and property of citizens, but should also endeavour to promote their welfare by some more positive action or interference on their behalf.'[4]

There are competing views about what governments should have the power to do in that respect. In an instrumental concept of government, government is there to do whatever is worth doing. Government, the conservative thinker Edmund Burke wrote, is 'a contrivance of human wisdom to provide for human wants.'[5] If a government wants to promote and subsidize activities such as opera, sport, gardening or broadcasting, that is up to them. The opposing stance is taken by constitutionalists: that a government can only legitimately do things that it is specifically and directly empowered to do. That is the mainstream view in the United States; its advocates see it as a restraint on the state, and a defence of liberal, individual values.[6]

A position related to constitutionalism is advocated by many on the political right, who take the view that action on welfare is liable to go beyond the legitimate authority of any government. 'Neoliberals', so called, assert the highly influential (but misguided) belief that governments are mainly there to do something else. Time and again, we are told that states are there to provide policing and defence, and that anything beyond that is questionable. 'The first duty of the sovereign', Adam Smith wrote in *The wealth of nations*, is 'that of protecting the society from the violence and invasion of other independent societies';[7] and Smith's dictum has been accepted as something that is so obvious it hardly needs to be discussed. Contemporary neoliberals have taken this as justification for a 'night-watchman' state, mainly confined to the limited roles of defence and public order: for example, Robert

Nozick, a 'libertarian' philosopher, suggests that a 'minimal state' should be based around a 'dominant protection agency'.[8] Some ideologues have found that appealing, but it is hardly consistent with the choices that governments make in practice. There has been a proliferation of new states and governments in the course of the last 30 to 40 years, and in so far as there is a common rationale, it has not been about defence; governments have been much more concerned with domestic policy, economic and social. The politicians, and the voters, want to be more prosperous. They want to be more like the richer countries.

Most democratic politicians, and (perhaps surprisingly) a fair number of undemocratic ones, see their job as trying to make people's lives better. The leading schools of thought promoting this view are liberalism and social democracy. Liberalism begins from individualist premises, but unlike contemporary neoliberalism (which promotes free markets, and tries to hold government activity to a minimum), liberal individualism allows governments some latitude about how they should go about their business. The 19th-century liberal John Stuart Mill, famously a powerful advocate for individual freedom, is often called on in support of arguments against paternalism. He argued that we should not intervene to stop people harming themselves, if they are determined to do so; that is something they should be free to do. However, he also wrote that 'When a government provides means of fulfilling a certain end, leaving individuals free to avail themselves of different means if in their opinion preferable, there is no infringement of liberty, no irksome or degrading restraint.'[9] Consent is fundamental to legitimacy. This has been a major liberal justification for health insurance, because we know from a range of histories that people will choose to have that insurance if they can afford it. The social insurance schemes of the Nordic countries, for example, developed on a voluntary basis, strongly influenced by trades unions and employment practices. They became compulsory only in the 1990s, partly to secure their financial position, but also to ensure that protection would extend to everyone.[10] (That, by the way, is one of the common justifications for compulsion: it is a way of making sure that no one is left out.)

The strongest support for state activity comes, however, from socialists. Socialism stands for the idea that government can make society better by applying collective moral principles – typically, the European socialist parties tell us, the values of liberty, equality, fraternity and democracy.[11] (Socialism is much misunderstood, usually deliberately. The mainstream of socialist thought in Europe is quite distinct from, and often directly opposed to, Marxism or communism. Marx sneered at the idea of a government of values, dismissing appeals to equal rights or fair distribution as 'obsolete verbal rubbish'.[12] Ethical socialists found that repellent, and communism and socialism parted company more than a century ago.) Clement Attlee, the Prime Minister when the British welfare state was founded, justified the policy in a call for human rights and social justice: 'The socialist appeal is essentially a moral one.'[13]

Arguments for welfare draw on a wider range of principles than those favoured by liberals and socialists, but clearly, there is likely to be some overlap; the process of developing welfare provision is shot through with moral values. The central point here is that the welfare state is much more than a matter of managing practical issues: government is a moral activity. This ties in closely with the idea of the welfare state discussed at the end of the first chapter. The 'welfare state' is an expression of a set of principles – not a menu of specific policies and prescriptions, but a guide to doing what is right.

3
THE AIMS OF SOCIAL WELFARE POLICIES

It should be clear, from what I have written so far, that any attempt to tie down the idea of the welfare state to a handful of specific services is doomed to failure. Nevertheless, it has to be acknowledged that many people do talk as if the welfare state is based on one simple principle – perhaps a safety net, possibly a clutch of cash benefits, maybe a general service to citizens. In this chapter, I will be discussing some of the main contenders.

The safety net

Any welfare state, if it is going to offer provision as of right, has to have some way of responding to people and contingencies that would otherwise be missed. This is one of the main guiding principles in the design of welfare systems. In many countries, welfare provision developed either as a form of mutual insurance, mainly covering people in formal employment, or as general provision for the population. Some developed countries have not gone far beyond that, and there are typically gaps in support for young people, homeless people, ex-prisoners or migrants.

On the face of the matter, this much should be uncontentious. There were people in the 19th century ready to argue that poor people should be made to suffer or left to die,[1] but hardly anyone nowadays would want seriously to make that case. The problems start when people argue that a safety net is all that a welfare state should do. 'Residual welfare' is based on the principle that most people will not need help. It is 'residual' because it deals with the 'residue', or leftovers – those people who cannot manage otherwise. Most people are supposed to meet their needs themselves, from their own or their family's resources. In Britain, this is strongly associated with the idea that the state should do the bare minimum, and perhaps less,[2] but that is not the only possible interpretation. In Australia, pensions are means-tested, but more than 90% of over-65s receive the pension. In Germany, high earners and self-employed people can opt out of the social insurance cover provided by the state. It's a question of where one draws the line.

Residual welfare is commonly developed, not as an all-embracing systemic response, but as a supplement to other services – a way of plugging holes in the net. There will always be a need for some provision of this kind, typically in combination with other more general services.[3] There are, however, many objections to residual welfare. Some reflect an unpopular history: residual systems have been associated with stigma, hardship and punitive measures taken against claimants. Some are concerned with method: the idea of supporting only the poorest and most needy calls for some way of distinguishing those who are eligible from those who are not, and there are major problems with equity, access, obtaining accurate information and managing claims. And some objections can be made in principle: that residual welfare makes invidious distinctions between people who receive benefits, for example for poverty, unemployment or disability, and those who do not.

In political discourse in Britain and America, you will come across repeated assertions that the welfare state began as a residual safety net, but that it has overreached itself. Charles Murray, a major critic of the expansion of 'welfare' in the USA, claimed that the original purpose of provision was to relieve poverty. 'Virtually all welfare expenditures went for cash grants and, with the most trivial exceptions, were spent on people whose indispensable claim to government help was that they had no job and no alternative means of support.'[4] In the UK, 'A system designed as a safety net for the most vulnerable has swelled into an all-consuming client state which stifles aspirations and dignity.'[5] Neither of these propositions stands up to scrutiny – they get the history wrong. In the USA, as a classic text points out, policies that are well-established and institutionalized, such as schooling, fire-fighting or drains, tend not to be thought of as 'welfare' at all.[6] When critics condemn the 'welfare state' for going beyond a safety net, they are probably not talking about waste disposal, child protection or old age pensions: they are pointing the finger at cash benefits for people of working age. In the UK, reliance on a residual safety net was just what the welfare state was supposed to replace. The welfare state made general provision, so that services for poor people would not be easily distinguishable from services for the rest of the population.

The great success of the welfare state has been to make acceptance of some major elements of provision so normal that they are hardly noticed, let alone questioned. The great failure has been of the attempt to extend that acceptance to other elements.

Protecting the vulnerable

Protecting people from what might happen goes some way beyond a safety net; it should, in principle, come into play before a safety net is needed. Part of the protection that is offered is protection from other people. In the same way as states protect people from violence, people may need to be protected from the behaviour of others in a broader sense – for example, social exclusion, debt or the impact of land ownership (which routinely denies some people access to shelter). Some of this is done through regulation and the establishment of rules, some through enforcement, some through legislation and civil action in the courts.[7]

For the United Nations, 'Social protection refers to policies designed to reduce people's exposure to risks, enhancing their capacity to protect themselves against hazards and loss of income.'[8] This is not quite right, because 'risk' is rather too broad a term. People are at risk if it is possible for bad things to happen; they are vulnerable if, when those things do happen, they are not able to cope with or overcome the effects. People can be at risk without being especially vulnerable – that is the common situation of people competing in business; they can be vulnerable without being seriously at risk, for example when they are in secure but low paid employment. Social protection is more typically concerned with vulnerability than with risk.

Vulnerability has many dimensions, some of which are hard to measure: the development expert Robert Chambers points to vulnerability through gender, subordination, exploitation and powerlessness.[9] A lack of resources is one of the main indicators; despite the limitations of the approach, that has led many to focus on cash assistance as a central strategy to ensure social protection. The International Labour Organization identifies social protection mainly with social security benefits: 'Social protection, or social security, provides benefits to individuals on the basis of risks faced across the life cycle (e.g., unemployment, disability, maternity, etc.) and to those suffering general poverty and social exclusion.'[10] The Asian Development Bank treats the principle as having a somewhat wider scope: they take the idea to include 'micro-and area-based schemes to address vulnerability at the community level, including microinsurance, agricultural insurance, social funds and programs to manage natural disasters; [or] child protection to ensure the healthy and productive development of children'.[11] The examples of child protection they refer to include not only financial assistance but programmes relating to child development, schooling, delinquency and street children. As the understanding of social protection broadens, it moves towards the kind of more extensive provision commonly associated with the welfare states.

Meeting needs and securing well-being

Needs, at the most basic level, are things that are required for human functioning, and without which people will be harmed. When people talk about needs, the focus tends initially to fall on the circumstances of individuals – needs for food, basic goods, warmth, shelter and so on – but it extends rapidly to other aspects of people's lives, such as participation in society, and to claims for service such as housing or medical care.[12]

There has been a tendency in some governments to treat the discussion of needs as if they only referred to a minimum set of physical needs, necessary for life and subsistence, but this is not true everywhere – there are other approaches, which work in different ways. One example is the use of comparative assessments of need: individuals and communities are compared to others who are less needy, and the numbers are used to determine the priorities. Another is based in the pattern of provision made by different services. People need food, but that is commonly treated as a demand for cash to buy food, rather than the supply of food as a good in its own right. A need for supportive care for older people becomes a claim for long-term residential care; a need for enhanced mobility might become a claim for public transport, or for private arrangements. In every society, the economist Amartya Sen argues, people are likely to be looking for ways to realize their 'capabilities', but the commodities that are available for them to do so will depend on the choices and patterns of life that apply in that society.[13]

The general aim of meeting needs is subject to an important reservation: there are many important, fundamental needs and aspects of well-being that are not in general seen as the province of the welfare state. People need love, affection, friendship, emotional support, imagination and play – life would be horrible without them – but they are not really what social welfare provision is about. In the context of social policy, people's needs are mainly concerned with a much more restricted category: harmful problems that imply a claim for services. There are some intriguing exceptions to that generalization – cases where social services have gone beyond the concept of need, and focussed on specific measures to enhance personal or communal well-being. Education services may well encourage personal development; health care services have on occasion been extended to offer people elective treatments, such as cosmetic surgery. More broadly, there may be a range of services and support that are not commonly thought of as part of the welfare state: engagement in sports, recreation, entertainment, broadcasting and cultural activities among them. It is disputable whether these can sensibly be thought of as the activities of a welfare state, but it is conceivable that, in some future time, they may be.

Redistribution

A fourth major set of issues focus on the redistributive aspects of the welfare state. Redistribution is commonly represented in two ways. Vertical redistribution is redistribution between people with more or less income. It is said to be 'progressive' if it goes from richer to poorer people, and 'regressive' if it goes from poorer to richer. Those are both shorthand labels, because in practice the effects of tax and spending may work in opposite directions for people at different points of the income distribution. Horizontal redistribution goes between people in different circumstances: pensions, for example, redistribute resources from people of working age to older people, and child benefits redistribute resources from people without children to families with them. Both those forms of horizontal redistribution might be viewed in a different way. From the perspective of the individual, the welfare state has the effect of redistributing resources over a person's lifetime: a 'piggy bank', economist Nick Barr suggests, rather than Robin Hood.[14]

Critics of redistributive policies usually represent the effect of welfare as a drain on the economy, and some critics have seen redistribution as an obstacle to the development of effective markets. Redistribution is rarely a drain on the economy, for a simple reason: if resources are being redistributed, that implies that the money is still there, only being spent by different people. Pensions and cash assistance are 'transfer payments'. This is commonly accounted for as if the money was being spent, but the money is not spent at the point of distribution. The whole point is that the recipients get the money so that they can spend it.

In economic terms, transfer payments should not make much difference to an economy – the amount of money in the economy remains the same. Pensions and social assistance should not have more than a marginal effect on overall performance, but there may be some specific effects. Poorer people spend more of their income than richer people, because they cannot save as much; that means that if they receive a redistributed income, there is likely to be a marginal stimulus to the demand for goods and services. They spend a higher proportion of their income on essential items, notably food; that can affect patterns of consumption overall. Both effects can be seen as potentially beneficial, both to the recipients and to the economy overall. The German 'ordo-liberals' promoted the idea of a 'social market economy'. They were opposed to the idea that the state might direct economic processes, but they sought to ensure that people would have a basic income through pensions and social security provision.[15] There is no conflict between those two positions. Any advocate of liberal, free markets should support a degree of redistribution: the markets have to be fuelled. If people have few or no resources, markets cannot thrive.

Public expenditure on social welfare services is implicitly redistributive, in the sense that those who pay are not the same as those who receive; any activity that is paid for by way of a welfare institution is unlikely to be done in the same proportions as the pre-existing distribution of income. With the main exception of benefits for people on very low incomes, it is debatable whether the redistribution associated with social welfare provision is necessarily purposeful: many of the patterns are the by-product of trying to have other effects. Primary schooling, for example, does tend to have a progressive, vertical effect, and public libraries, which are used more by the better educated, tend to have a slightly regressive impact,[16] but it is very questionable whether such effects are central to the role of either. Something else is going on. Richard Tawney, a socialist writer, made a case for viewing public expenditure in a different way. The point of redistribution is

> not the division of the nation's income into [millions of] fragments, to be distributed, without further ado, like cake at a school treat ... It is to make accessible to all, irrespective of their income, occupation or social position, the conditions of civilisation which, in the absence of such measures, can only be enjoyed by the rich.[17]

That, to my mind, is a much better characterization of redistribution in the welfare states than the idea that they are mainly a system of transfers from rich to poor.

This should help to clarify one of the points about redistributive policy which seems to confuse academic commentators. The problem has been called the 'Robin Hood paradox'. Why, the question runs, is there less redistribution in societies which are more unequal? Surely, if needs are greater, there ought to be more redistribution, not less?[18] The answer to that question is that it's never really been about redistribution to individuals. It's about public services, social infrastructure and the 'conditions of civilisation'. Needs are greater when those services aren't available. Countries which have less developed services have further to go.

Social security

Social security is often represented as a form of insurance; people effectively pool their risk, so that the impact of bad experiences will not lead to severe consequences. That is the basic rationale behind health insurance (which, in many countries, is thought of as a social security benefit, rather than a health benefit as such).

Some forms of insurance began with mutual aid. Some large insurance companies began life as non-profit institutions; there are still fields of activity, such as funeral insurance, where that tradition continues. In a commercial market, people join insurance schemes for all kinds of reasons – some because it is prudent, some because they want to minimize the risks they face, some because it is a way of protecting families and survivors, some because coverage is made easy for them. The contribution of mutual insurance was recognized by many governments, and the growth of social insurance secured by government has become a major element in the finance of social welfare programmes.

Part of that process, however, has been that governments found themselves engaging with schemes that were incomplete, and liable to miss in particular the people on the lowest incomes. The development of such schemes in France is illustrative. As the country industrialized, people who were employed often had the opportunity to join a scheme within the network of organizations offering pensions and medical benefits. When it came to the reform of benefits after World War II, however, only half the employed population was covered. The French government wanted to build on the existing networks. Pierre Laroque, the main architect of the reforms, explained:

> No system of social security is viable if it does not respond to national traditions, if it does not respond to the economic and psychological circumstances of the country. Now, the French tradition in the domain of social security is not a tradition of state bureaucracy. It's a tradition of voluntary mutual support. It's a tradition of a selfless effort and generous mutual insurance. It's a tradition of mutualism. It's the tradition of syndicalism. It's the tradition of the old French socialism. ... It's that tradition which has its

name inscribed in our national motto – it's the tradition
of fraternity.[19]

The gradual extension of the *régime général* took the
best part of thirty years; and when the scheme was
finally complete, the authorities realized that there
were still five million people left without coverage.[20]
At that point, the French government began to seek
options for further extension of provision, in the form
of social inclusion.

Solidarity and inclusion

The idea of 'solidarity' is widely misunderstood
in English-speaking texts, but for many people in
continental Europe it represents the most fundamental
principle underlying social welfare provision. Solidarity
is commonly thought of, in English, as a sentiment:
people 'express solidarity' by going on demonstrations
or making approving noises.[21] Try to forget that,
because it is irrelevant to welfare. What is relevant is a
rather different, and much more substantial, meaning of
the term. The teaching of the Catholic Church refers to
the principle as 'A firm and persevering determination
to commit oneself to the common good, that is ... the
good of all and of each individual, because we are all
responsible for each other.'[22] Solidarity refers to mutual
responsibility – the networks of shared obligation and
support that are the substance of most of our social
relations. 'Solidarity', the historian Peter Baldwin
explains, 'is the child of interdependence.'[23] The growth

of mutual aid and forms of social protection are a part of those processes.

This leads directly to the concepts of exclusion and inclusion. People are said to be 'marginal' when they are not fully integrated into solidaristic systems of support, and 'excluded' when they are outside them.[24] Exclusion happens when people are left out (because there are no systems of support, or 'holes in the net'); kept out, because they are not thought of as members of a society (for example, the position of migrants); or pushed out, the effect of stigma and social rejection. One of the principal roles of state provision has been to include more people – extending the advantages of solidarity to those who would otherwise not be fully part of society.

Solidarity is important both for individuals, and for the communities they live in. One of the objectives associated with solidarity is the promotion of social cohesion; social relations are an important constituent of people's well-being. 'By and large', Boulding wrote, 'it is an objective of social policy to build the identity of a person around some community with which he is associated.'[25] Social cohesion can be understood in many ways. The Council of Europe refers to definitions based on social bonds (for example, 'the promotion of stable, co-operative and sustainable communities'); shared values and a sense of belonging ('the ongoing process of developing a community of shared values, shared challenges and equal opportunities based on a sense of hope, trust and reciprocity'); and the ability to live and work together in harmonious co-existence: 'Social cohesion is defined as the capacity of citizens living under different social or economic circumstances to live together in harmony, with a sense of mutual commitment.'[26]

These expressions are mainly positive, but solidarity does have a downside. The same processes which shape our obligations and our social identity can act to exclude outsiders – people who are not part of the network of obligations and rights that unify the rest. Many of the dilemmas faced by contemporary welfare states are concerned with social inclusion – finding ways to draw people in to networks of support and obligation.

Citizenship and social rights

The sociologist TH Marshall identified social rights with a model of citizenship that would apply equally to everyone. 'Citizenship', he wrote, 'is a status bestowed on those who are full members of a community. All those who possess the status are equal with respect to the rights and duties with which the status is endowed'.[27] Social citizenship seems to imply that everyone will benefit from a common set of legal rights – that is, general or universal claims, backed up by law. The implication is that no one should be left behind – a right to welfare should be more inclusive than solidarity alone.[28] However, the idea of citizenship suffers, like the idea of solidarity, from the problem of exclusion. If the right to welfare is based on membership of a community, there must be those who are not considered members, and so who are not citizens.

The social rights associated with citizenship – such as rights to health care, housing or social protection – are not 'human rights'. Human rights refer to an irreducible minimum, available to everyone, whoever they are and wherever they may be. The rights of citizenship, which have been much more important in the development of welfare,[29] are there for the members of a specific society. When the Inter-American Human Rights Court considered the human rights of five Peruvian pensioners who were being denied their pension, the judges passed over the submission that this was a 'grave violation of the human right of social security' and opted to treat the issue instead as a denial of specific property rights.[30] Despite the rhetoric, the 'right to welfare' is neither a right to everything, nor a right for everyone.

The principle of social citizenship has been influential, but it offers very little guidance as to what rights might mean in practice. 'Equal status' implies a 'right to have rights', providing a foundation for every claim of right in the future. However, the rights that people hold are not rights to equal things; what people are entitled to depends on their circumstances. As Marshall recognized, rights are hemmed in with conditions and restrictions. Many of the rights that people have in contemporary societies are not universal at all. They are particular: that is, they are distinctive and apply only to the person who holds them. In many welfare states, pensions are based in particular rather than general rights; they are related to individual contributions and entitlements that differ person by person. The biggest and most secure pension systems in Europe depend on that principle, which should give us pause for thought. People are not always best served by universal rules.

Social investment

In recent years some writers have advanced the idea that welfare states ought to take the form of 'social investment', aiming to enhance welfare by taking a long-term view of people's development and place in society.[31] Hemerijck, one of the leading advocates of this approach, emphasizes three roles in particular: investing in the 'stock' of people; regulating 'flows' as people go through different stages in the life-cycle; and providing 'buffers', that is, protection in times of need.[32] The concept is already wide, and there are many forms of state action that can be interpreted as long-term 'investment'. They include, in part, doing things to the advantage of long-term economic development, such as enhancing the skills and potential contribution that people are able to make to the economy; in part, by improving 'human capital', education and training, 'capacitation' or increasing the productive potential of families;[33] and building 'social capital', the common benefit that people derive from being in social networks in a developed society. The concept of social investment has been cited in support of promoting gender equity, ensuring the long-term sustainability of welfare institutions; taking action, such as early child care or disease prevention, to prevent later harms; and stabilizing a society in the face of common risks.

It is difficult to say whether any of this does genuinely represent a distinctive paradigm or new set of objectives for welfare. Its advocates commonly refer to the need to adapt to 'new' social risks, but for the most part the risks they are talking about – such as poverty, exclusion, precarious livelihoods or outdated skills – are issues that have been evident for centuries. The concept has been criticized for its emphasis on the formal labour market, and its apparent effect in supporting families that are already better-off than others.[34]

Supporting the economy

In the main, the support that governments give to the economy is based in economic policies, not social ones, but the boundaries are fuzzy. Some economic policies straddle social policy: fiscal policy, including tax rates and allowances, agricultural subsidies, labour market policies and regional policies among them. It is no less true that the provision of social welfare services might be seen as an enhancement to the economy. Schooling equips children with the basic skills they will need as adult workers, and provides child care that releases parents to work. Health services help to maintain a healthy workforce. More generally, the economist Joseph Stiglitz suggests that because welfare protects people from adverse risks, that makes it easier for them to take risks and innovate.[35]

There are those who think that economy and social welfare are diametrically opposed: in the 1970s, one of the most influential books on the economic problems of the UK argued that private production was fundamental, and that public expenditure always represented a drain on the economy.[36] The assumption being made here is that private business is productive, and public spending is not. Both sides of that argument are off-beam: some private business is 'rent-seeking' or parasitic, and public enterprise is often necessary for economic development.[37] Policies which have been based on like assumptions have a chequered history. The efforts of the World Bank and the International Monetary Fund to require 'structural adjustment' in the 1980s and '90s were intended to change the balance of public and private sectors, seeking to encourage the development of markets through privatization and reducing state activity. This approach had mixed results at best, with some countries experiencing severe hardship as a result.[38]

The belief that states make things worse, and that the private sector will make them better, has sometimes got in the way of sound economic management. Some eminent economists have laid into it,[39] but it is still influential. The World Bank, for example, tells us: 'it is not the role of governments to create jobs ... as a general rule it is the private sector that creates jobs'.[40] That is nonsense; it clearly is part of the role of government to create jobs. States routinely create jobs for police officers, teachers, refuse collectors, soldiers, fire fighters, social workers and civil servants, to name but a few. The jobs of other workers in the private sector may well depend on work commissioned by governments: examples can be found among workers on roads, health workers, transport, child care, criminal lawyers, farmers and so on. Creating employment is one of the main routes by which welfare states can contribute to economic development. The proper test is whether the government is doing this well, not whether it is doing it at all.

Changing behaviour

The most obvious way in which governments attempt to change people's behaviour is through the criminal law, punishing behaviours that are disapproved of. They can try to produce effects in many other ways, such as regulation, education, propaganda and persuasion. Governments offer rewards for approved behaviour or sanctions for conditions that are disapproved of. In this respect, social welfare provision can become an instrument for governing people. Welfare provision has often been accused of being a way of enforcing 'social control' – imposing a moral order, punishing deviant behaviour and asserting a dominant authority.[41] There are circumstances in which the effect on people's welfare is secondary to a broader aim – for example, promoting childbirth or participation in the labour market – but equally, there may be attempts to change behaviour in the belief that this will lead to better welfare, such as health promotion in relation to diet or smoking, or the attempts to make cash support conditional on sending children to school.

Some economic measures are taken with the intention of shaping behaviour, by introducing 'incentives' or 'disincentives'. The arguments around such policies are muddled. Economists used to argue that they were dealing with aggregate populations, not individual choices. If people are offered an inducement to change their behaviour, some (and only some) within the total population may do so. The extent to which they will actually do so is represented by the concept of 'elasticity', which records people's aggregate responsiveness to a stimulus. Some options will be chosen by many; some, by hardly anyone. That way of thinking makes sense, but it goes with a warning: sometimes the options on offer are not ones people will choose. Developing inducements to have more children has been happening in many countries with plummeting birth rates, usually with little effect. Women are having fewer children, and having them later, because they are making other choices in life.[42] Some women may be persuaded by financial inducements, but the elasticity is limited: the money is not enough to produce the desired effect, and it is unclear if any amount would be.

In economic studies of the welfare state, unfortunately, the assessment of incentives has largely been abandoned in favour of 'rational choice' theory, and that approach has at best a tenuous relationship to reality.[43] A 'rational choice' is supposedly the choice that will be made by a notional, clear-thinking individual who is determined to pursue self-interest. People are supposed to respond predictably to stimuli: sticks and carrots, Charles Murray tells us, work. On that basis, people who receive benefits will choose to be unemployed and do nothing, instead of taking a job.[44] But sticks and carrots don't work, not in the way that Murray imagines. There are two immediate problems. The first is that the application of rational choice theory depends on the assumption that 'other things are equal', and they never are. The effect of an 'incentive' cannot be understood in isolation; people do not respond simply because a benefit is laid in front of them. The second is that choices have consequences; they lead to costs as well as benefits. Those costs can include time, physical discomfort, stress, anxiety, stigma and loss of personal autonomy. Beyond that, there is always an 'opportunity cost' – the sacrifice of the option that is not being taken. From the point of view of the individual, an inducement is not going to work as an incentive if the costs of a choice exceed the benefits. The costs of being unemployed can be massive – not just income foregone, but dealing with bureaucracy, sanctions, social isolation, poverty and longer-term disadvantage. The claim that unemployment benefits are an incentive to become unemployed is not much more plausible, on the face of the matter, than a suggestion that funeral payments are an incentive to die. The claim to the contrary is thoroughly bad economics – or it would be, if economic theory was the true motivation for the punitive treatment of welfare recipients. It probably isn't.

The welfare state as a means to an end

The emphasis on changing behaviour points to another aspect of social welfare provision. At times, the delivery of services is not the main consideration. Many governments justify their engagement in welfare as a means to an end. Welfare might be a means of achieving political objectives – for example, forging a sense of national identity, promoting a religious grouping or a particular set of values, or justifying the authority of a party in power. Social policy may be seen as a tool to change society, for example by striving for equality – or possibly, the opposite. The contrast is striking in different responses to the position of women – some states have actively promoted equality, while others have imposed huge restrictions on women's participation in society. Iran, for example, has contrived to develop a range of systems for social protection at the same time as it represses women's basic freedoms.[45]

At times, too, the welfare state has been represented as a staging post on the way to a new society – the 'New Jerusalem', perhaps, or some other Utopia. Tony Crosland, an influential socialist politician, was withering about the search for ideal states. The fundamental problem, he argued, is that any step which is supposedly taken towards the ideal must, if it has any effect, change the conditions that the policy was intended to address.

> We can ... describe the direction of advance, and even discern the immediate landscape ahead; but the ultimate objective lies wrapped in complete uncertainty. This must

> be the case unless one subscribes to the vulgar fallacy
> that some ideal society can be said to exist, of which
> blueprints can be drawn, and which will be ushered in as
> soon as certain specific reforms have been achieved ...
> in Western societies change is gradual and evolutionary,
> and not always either foreseeable of even under political
> control. ... We must re-assess the matter in the light of
> every new situation.[46]

This is as much a criticism of planned reform in stages as
it is of revolutionary change. Utopias are self-defeating.

The many objectives of welfare states

It is evidently wrong to say that the welfare state is
only a safety net; its scope is much broader. It is no less
misleading to say that the welfare state is a response
to needs – it only ever responds to some of them. If
the welfare state is to be understood as an engine of
redistribution, it is not always very good at it. And it is
difficult to argue that the welfare state is only concerned
with supporting the economy: it does in some ways,
but not to the exclusion of other objectives.

Which of these approaches can be applied, then, to
welfare states? The quick answer is, all of them, but
in different permutations. Focusing on only one of
these objectives, to the exclusion of the others, would
imply that something important is being forgotten.
The welfare state is not a single service, working to
a simple, unified objective. Different services work to
different criteria. Social workers, particularly those in

child protection, are generally concerned with risk; health workers with medical priority; housing officers with fairness, and sometimes with protecting settled communities; teachers with personal development. If we 'drill down' to consider the operation of different services, we will find that the same sense of diversity in aims and approaches permeates the provision of social welfare at many levels.

Some of the objectives of social services can be tied directly to the broad, generic aims already considered – a safety net, a response to need, an aid to economic development, and so on. But that does not exhaust all the considerations.

Consider the objectives of health care. In the first instance, those objectives include several which have already been considered in this chapter: providing a safety net, protecting the vulnerable, meeting needs, solidarity, social investment, supporting the economy (by maintaining a healthy workforce), security and the right to welfare.

Beyond that, however, there are yet more objectives:

- *The protection of some from the actions of others.* Governments commonly engage with provision in such areas as the regulation of food quality, or restraining the excessive use of antibiotics, because that will diminish their effectiveness.
- *Public health.* This includes preventive actions such as vaccination, the control of infectious diseases, sanitation and environmental protection. One of the key aspects of public health is that it is not only

done for the benefit of individuals; it is necessary for whole community.

- *Enhancing individual well-being.* A range of elective procedures might be undertaken, not just to protect people from ill health, but to enhance their lives. Those procedures currently extend to cosmetic surgery, infertility treatments, gender reassignment and religious circumcision.
- *Supporting the interests of health care providers.* This one may be unexpected, because it is not focused on the needs of the people being served, but there is international competition for the services of health care professionals, and failures to maintain the infrastructure – training the necessary staff, offering appropriate terms and conditions and providing the necessary equipment – can have a disruptive effect on the maintenance of health care.

Let's move on to the aims of education services. They share with health services some objectives that were discussed earlier in this chapter: meeting needs; solidarity; the right to welfare; social investment – in this case, by developing human capital, training and the development of skills; and supporting the economy, by social investment and by providing a child-minding service.

Educational services might also be thought to include some other aims:

- *Promoting individual achievement.* Liberal education stands for the development of each individual intellectually and socially to that person's fullest potential.

- *Integration into society*. Education is a method of transmission of social norms and values, a process of 'socialization'.
- *Social control*. There is a 'hidden curriculum': children are taught how to behave, including deference to authority.
- *Promoting or preserving a culture*. Education is an important vehicle for appreciation of, and the continuation of interest in, language, history, music and art.
- *Innovation*. Higher education is the well-spring of research, science and social development.
- *Maintaining or changing society*. The education system has been seen both as a way of reinforcing social relations and as a means of bringing about social change. This is sometimes referred to as 'social engineering'.

Turning to social security benefits, several of the generic aims considered so far in this chapter are most likely to be identified with supplementing low income. They include providing a safety net; social protection; meeting needs; solidarity; economic management, by assisting and smoothing the labour market, and stimulating the economy when economic activity is low; redistribution; changing behaviour; providing security; and asserting the right to welfare.

That is already more elements than either health or education, but there are still more uses for cash benefits. They include:

- *Excusing people from the obligation to work*. This one may be surprising, when so many countries have been introducing so-called 'activation' in order to require the opposite. The point of putting it this way is to acknowledge that the core structure of benefits for retirement, sickness and maternity is designed precisely to make it possible for people to withdraw from the labour market, whether that is for short periods or, in the cases of incapacity or retirement, indefinitely.

- *Supporting other services*. A range of cash benefits are used to encourage people to engage with health or education services. This is explicit in the Conditional Cash Transfers introduced in a number of developing countries – the 'condition' is that parents report for health monitoring or ensure that their children go to school.

- *Compensation*. There may be schemes to compensate people for government actions, such as war disability pensions or payments for vaccine damage. One of the most commonly legislated forms of cash benefit is the provision of compensation for industrial injury.

- *Financing particular activities*. Social security benefits have been used to channel spending on rented housing, residential care for older people, and food production – the last of these being part of the rationale, in the USA, for food stamps.

The aims of social services are unavoidably complex. As the focus moves to the fine grain of policy, simplistic generalizations about the purpose of welfare become harder to sustain. This all points, in my view, to the absurdity of trying to classify and pigeonhole welfare states in terms of regimes. There are far too many claims to balance or activities to consider, and too much diversity within those activities.

4
THE CASE FOR WELFARE

Why do so many governments think it right to be engaged with social welfare provision? What's the point? The first answers to those questions are based in morality: a view that the provision of welfare is the right thing to do. Second, there are common interests, that need a collective response to be addressed. Third, there are economic rationales. And fourth, there are material advantages to be gained, for those in government as well as those who receive services. This chapter will look at each of those in turn.

Moral purposes

Some moral arguments are based in statements of principle, such as religious precepts and secular moral codes. It is quite common for history books to attribute the development of welfare services to a religious spirit, such as charity or compassion.[1] That emphasis is tenable, because often religious institutions were there first, but it is selective – charitable provision has often been developed at the same time as other forms of welfare, such as patronage, mutual aid or attempts to control society. Religious morality has certainly had a profound effect on the way that social welfare works in practice. That may be expressed as a general approval of benevolence. Religious charity is usually understood as a duty to God, rather than a right of the person who receives it: the difference is both a marker of status and a question of accountability. Organized religion also led, however, to the adoption of quite specific rules in the major religions about how resources should be distributed in a community, what should be included and who should have the duty to do it. The governance of charitable trusts was typically established under the auspices of the religious authorities; as modern states developed, this was to set some of the patterns for the conduct of government, such as audit and accountability.[2] Mediaeval confraternities offered mutual support, public charity and religious justification as part of the same package.[3] It becomes difficult, then, to distinguish religious purposes from other considerations.

It could be said that general principles such as altruism and humanitarianism have the same characteristics as religious charity, but they are broader. Humanitarianism, as the name suggests, is supposed to cover common humanity. Altruism, less precisely, encompasses any provision that is made for the benefit of other people. Often that is expressed in specific social contexts.

Altruism is sometimes dismissed, because people rarely act in ways that are free of all considerations of self-interest, but that is not important. Altruism can work in everyone's favour, for those who give as well as those who receive. From sociology and anthropology, detailed studies and theoretical arguments have been made in respect of the 'norm of reciprocity'.[4] Simple reciprocity, or 'balanced exchange', is widespread and recognizable in many cultures: but so is 'generalized' reciprocity, where returns are indirect and a balance may never be arrived at. Parents and children typically have relationships reflecting both balanced and generalized reciprocity. Balanced reciprocity can be seen in the feeling that as parents look after their children when they are young, the children should look after their parents when they are old. That is only part of the story. Parents look after children in part because their parents looked after them – that is an example of generalized reciprocity. They have other generalized obligations to their parents because of what their parents did for the preceding generation. Children look after aged parents because those parents supported the child's grandparents. The different principles all apply at the same time, binding people into social relationships to an astonishing extent. Richard Titmuss argued that the principle of 'gift-exchange' was pervasive. Every act of altruism contributes to the pattern of duties and responsibilities which make up a society.[5] When it comes to social protection, it is often possible to see it as an extension of the same principle: the circumstances which lead people to draw on pensions, health insurance or unemployment benefits are the sorts of condition that anyone might experience, and it makes sense to share in mutually beneficial networks of reciprocity.

If we look at the question of who else these obligations are directed towards, it often comes out in terms of a basic obligation for rich people to help poor people. The anthropologist Marshall Sahlins suggests that the sense of mutual obligation is fundamental to the very existence of a society; if societies have nothing that binds together rich and poor people, he argues, they cease to be societies.[6] At the same time, however, it is evident that obligations are not only directed to the poor. There is usually a clear sense that people have responsibilities to others who are taken to be dependent – children, elderly people or people with disabilities. There are commitments and obligations that people have to people closer to them – their family, their community, their networks. And there are special cases, such as the victims of natural disasters or wars, which may reasonably be taken as evidence of an obligation to humanity in more general terms.

Altruism is not, by any means, the only test of ethical conduct. Many participants in a political discourse will choose to refer to other principles: values such as freedom or fairness, claims about the beneficial consequences of policies, appeals to virtuous conduct in relation to religion or family life. The standards being applied are vague. It can be difficult to anticipate just who is going to be the object of other people's moral concern, and who might be set aside. Why are refugees from one war given special consideration, when people from a different war have no priority? Why should industrial injuries be protected, when someone with the self-same injury from other causes is not? Why do some countries provide extensive child care, while others have little? Don't ask for consistency, a former political adviser warns us; that is not how policy works.

> In the seminar room the appeal to inconsistency is perhaps the strongest argument we have. ... No one should hold an inconsistent position. But in public policy this does not work so well. ... Ideally, of course, there would be no inconsistencies, but many laws are compromises between competing interests, and different laws are made by different people, at different times for different purposes. While one can hope for consistency it would be foolish to expect it.[7]

The factors that make an issue salient enough to call for action – that make people say, 'something must be done' – depend on much more than consideration of moral arguments: for example, political priorities, press scrutiny, perceived costs and competing claims. Social policy, notoriously, has often been driven by the experience of war – famous examples include the foundation of the British welfare state or the French *régime général*. (The two are connected. In the UK, the Beveridge report promised a 'British revolution' after the war. Copies of that report were parachuted into France as propaganda, and the National Council of the Resistance produced a plan directly influenced by it.[8]) In peacetime, scandal has arguably played a greater part in bringing problems to public notice than research ever has – for example, in revealing problems of child abuse, or the abuse of psychiatric patients in mental hospitals. Even if moral principles play a part, they are rarely the whole story.

The common good

Morality might be, at times, boiled down to the question of who benefits; if moral precepts are based on the consequences of our actions, it should be possible to decide on the merits of a policy by asking what those policies achieve. 'Consequentialist' morality, such as utilitarian thought, takes actions to be good if they have, or are intended to have, good consequences. If, however, welfare only benefits some people at the expense of others, collective action for welfare becomes a trade-off of one person's rights against another's. Thinking about benefits and services in that way has usually been the focus of commentators who are opposed to welfare, seeing it as a public burden. It may be all right to support a few deserving cases, the argument runs, but we don't want people to be unemployed at the expense of hard-working taxpayers. If we want to justify social policies in other terms, we need to think about benefits and services differently.

The arguments for seeing protection as part of a common good are of two kinds. The first is that the protection is mutual: if anyone can find themselves in a situation where they need help, mutual provision adds to everyone's security and well-being. The other justification is collective. Welfare services benefit not just the individual recipients, but the whole community.

Welfare states can be taken to support a mixture of individual and collective social principles. The arguments underlying those positions are complex – too complex for this short book – but the values are not. For individuals, the welfare state offers the protection of a range of common standards, including the rights of citizenship, minimum income standards and political rights; the protection of common interests, such as emergency services, medical care and access to information; basic security through medical care, public health and child protection; and protection against common social risks.[9] For the broader society, welfare states offer collective action to achieve collective benefit: solidarity, socialization, stewardship for future generations, democracy, participation and empowerment in decisions, or collective security.[10] There is no guarantee that any of these objectives will be realized in full, but the broad patterns should be recognizable. These are things that just about all developed societies have been trying to do.

Within that very rough framework, there are three main interpretations of what a 'common good' might be. The first, which is still very much centred on people as 'individuals', takes it to mean that some individuals gain, and others do not. Governments often focus either on national income or on GDP, the Gross Domestic Product, which is not quite but nearly the same thing. There is an implicit assumption that people are gaining from increases in GDP, a tendency to dismiss the contribution made by government;[11] and a somewhat cavalier assertion (known to economists as the 'Kaldor-Hicks' criterion) that if the winners have the resources to compensate the losers, then everyone is really better off, even if this 'compensation' never happens. There is a lot wrong with GDP as a test. Some things are counted, such as a child leaving school early to scrape a living; other things, such as women's domestic labour, are hardly counted at all. Some things that are counted are bad things, of the sort that governments really shouldn't want to encourage: drugs, prostitution, crime. And other things that are counted are 'anti-bads', such as spending on policing, prisons and public order – they increase GDP when things get worse.

A second view of the common good focuses on shared interests, or 'common ground': the things that affect people collectively, not just individually. Public goods, such as roads and street lighting, are examples. The principle can be taken more widely, however; what matters here is that people have interests in common. Some common interests are there because welfare delivers extra benefits for society, such as the gain to everyone from better health or education. Some are there because some things can only be achieved through people doing those things in concert, or together. The facilities open to people in a locality, such as medical care, banking and schools, necessarily depend on the numbers of people who are being served; the lack of sufficient numbers is often a problem in remote and rural areas. And some are there because of socialization, that is, because people have learned to appreciate them as part of social life: the enjoyment of theatre, sport and music depends on a social infrastructure that makes these things possible. People hold these shared interests at the same time as they hold their own personal interests.

The third sense of the common good refers to things that are purely collective – things that are good for a society, rather than a specific set of its citizens. Foreign policy, defence and international relations, all part of the 'national interest', are examples that even diehard individualists usually accept. It is not much of a stretch to accept that a whole society is also better off if there are houses, schools, hospitals, water supplies, sanitation and so forth. Decent sewers benefit everyone. In 19th-century Britain, there were debates between those who wanted to approve the installation of sewers and those who resented the cost. (Lord Palmerston dubbed the opposition 'the dirty party'.) There is no real contradiction here – people can have individual and collective interests at the same time. People often have competing individual interests – for example, they might have to choose between leisure and personal development. In the same way, they can have a balance of individual interests leading in one direction, and a share in the collective interests that leads in another. The question that governments have to resolve is when, and in what circumstances, interests shared by everyone should be preferred to the interests of individuals.

The main difficulty here is to know how to identify the interests of a whole society. Some writers have argued for a sense of 'public values':

> Public values are those providing normative consensus about (1) the rights, benefits, and prerogatives to which citizens should (and should not) be entitled; (2) the obligations of citizens to society, the state and one another; and (3) the principles on which governments and policies should be based.[12]

Consensus is easier to claim than to find, but there is a case for considering communal values as issues in their own right, which I will return to in the next chapter.

Economic purposes

In some models, the welfare state is seen as a mainstay of a 'capitalist' economy – developing human capital, maintaining society, preparing a trained workforce and promoting social integration. The same arguments, however, can also be the source of criticism. Modern economies work to the benefit of those who already have most, and supporting the economy can be seen, in another light, as reinforcing existing inequalities. The political scientist Christopher Pierson examines several propositions about the welfare state: among them, that it was part of the evolution of modern capitalism, that it does not fit with the new globalism, that it is a compromise between class interests, that the welfare state has been a temporary solution to problems, that it is no longer needed, or that it is an obstacle to progress.[13]

This is all built around the idea that the 'economic system' works in an integrated, purposeful way, summed up by the label, 'capitalism', and that 'the welfare state' represents another integrated, purposeful system pulling in the opposite direction. The world is just not like this. 'Capitalism' is a crudely drawn term, used to talk about any sort of contemporary economic activity: the same word is used to cover large corporations, manufacturers, financiers, independent artisans, mutuals, shopkeepers, farmers, feudal landlords, social enterprises and any other economic process that springs to mind. The idea of the 'welfare state' is equally used to describe a huge range of social and institutional arrangements, covering state and non-state actors alike, with a vast array of aims and purposes.

Many welfare services do help the economy. Education, health and social assistance all help to promote economic development – that is certainly a primary justification for education services and other investment in human capital. 'Human capital' is a way of thinking about the potential contribution of people to the economy, and perhaps a device used to sneak human issues in to discussions of economic policies: developing women's rights is a splendid way of doing both.

No less than defence or foreign policy, economic development is commonly conceived as a matter of national interest, but it is more contentious – in the economy, there are always winners and losers. That means that development is not an unalloyed good. In many developing countries, economic development has led to a growing formal economy, urbanization and higher incomes. By 2030, the United Nations estimates, 60% of the world's population will be living in cities. The trend is most visible in the growth of the world's 'megacities' – urban regions with populations of at least ten million, more than many small countries. Most of the world's megacities are now in Asia or Africa: among the largest, where there are more than twenty million inhabitants, are Delhi and Mumbai in India, Shanghai and Beijing in China. Other massive megacities in emerging economies include Mexico City and São Paulo in Brazil, and a similar process has led to the growth of megacities in poorer countries, such as Dhaka in Bangladesh and Kinshasa in the Democratic Republic of the Congo. The shift to cities is a clear sign of development – but the same shift has also led to insecurity, the breakup of rural communities and some serious inequalities.

The other thing about economic development is that it never stops: once a country is 'developed', the issue will be called 'growth' instead. Like a shark, an economy has to keep moving forwards, or it will die. The reason why is that part of economic activity is made up of 'primary production', the production of goods and services which are necessary for other goods and services to grow and develop. If the economy is not growing, the demand for primary production falls, usually some time before other industry, and so growth falters. It may be theoretically possible to run an economy that is self-regulating, static and holds all production and demand in a permanent balance, but if so no one has worked out how.

Political advantage

Last but not least, we need to consider another benefit of developing a welfare state: that it works directly to the advantage of self-interested governments. Eibl, in *Social dictatorships*, describes arrangements across a swathe of countries in the Middle East and North Africa, with a particular emphasis on Tunisia and Egypt. Many of the states that make provision for their populations are run by self-seeking autocrats, who have used their command of welfare systems to entrench their authority and mobilize support. Creating jobs in the public sector is particularly favoured as a method of rewarding supporters. Eibl describes this support as an 'authoritarian support coalition'.[14]

This could be taken to be a cynical, and perhaps sinister, manipulation of the citizenry. There are two reasons to discount that. The first is that electoral democracies do the same. There has been a bewildering array of explanations for the expansion of welfare services in middle-income democracies: they include, among others, economic performance, electoral competition, partisan ideology, labour unions, social movements and cultural influences.[15] The upshot is, perhaps predictably, that any of these can plausibly be presented as helping to drive democratic countries towards the expanded provision. When a political party or presidential candidate makes their offer to the electorate, what are they doing if it is not a way of persuading people to vote for them? The electoral process has a profound effect on the conduct of governments. They have to offer something to the electorate, or at least to a sufficiently large portion of the electorate, to win or to maintain themselves in power. Amartya Sen argues that there has never been a famine in a democracy.[16] This is arguable – it all depends how one defines a democracy – but the gist is persuasive; democratic governments need to do enough to mobilize support, and cannot maintain their position if they alienate a large enough proportion of people.

The second reservation concerns legitimacy. Legitimacy is fundamental to a government's authority. Critics have complained that it may be a sham: Jürgen Habermas, a writer strongly influenced by Marxism, writes of a 'legitimation crisis' when the development of welfare provision comes into conflict with the accumulation of capital.[17] The thing about a claim to legitimacy, however, is that it changes the way that governments, and their supporters, act. Some flawed governments, like Jordan or Bangladesh, have done a lot to secure the welfare of their people, and – without wishing to condone their conduct in other respects – to my mind that makes them better governments than North Korea or Myanmar. Governments which do things to benefit their populations are not just pretending to be more legitimate: they are more legitimate.

The opposition

We have arrived, then, at a point where it becomes very clear why governments should want their countries to become welfare states, or at least engage in the sorts of activity that are thought of as welfare states. The reasoning is moral, pragmatically beneficial, economic and political. These arguments are simply overwhelming, and that is why governments in almost every country in the world, regardless of their ideological inclinations, accept them to some degree. It is harder to understand why any government should not want to do this.

Opposition to the welfare state is nothing new. Much of it depends on the particular constructions that people put on the idea of the welfare state: that it is not a proper use of the powers of government and the state, or that it is a staging post to an all-powerful state that the opponents don't wish to see. No less forceful are the complaints that the actions of welfare services corrupt and destroy the motivation of the recipients of welfare. Last but not least, the welfare states are castigated for their supposed failures – the excessive expense and the way they undermine the operation of a private market. Oftentimes, these criticisms are made all at once, in an unending salvo of curses and prophecies of doom.

The first set of objections is based in a restrictive view of the purposes and powers of governments. That could be based in a constitutional stance, that governments and states can only have those powers which are directly granted to them;[18] to the argument that individuals have rights, such as rights to property, which states cannot legitimately set aside;[19] or that states cannot legitimately do things that are in people's interests, because that undermines individual freedom of action.[20] The direct responses to these points are that governments can, if desired, be invested with the powers they lack; that there is no good reason to suppose that property rights trump all the others; and that securing basic decency and access to the conditions of civilization does not undermine people's freedom of action, it enhances it. The other argument, that welfare leads down the 'road to serfdom',[21] does not deserve to be taken seriously: decisions to support health care or pensions are not the first steps towards tyranny. The argument that this is a 'slippery slope' is akin to the argument that we should never walk westward, because if we go far enough we'll all drown.

The second parcel of objections stems from the idea that welfare changes, not just how people behave, but what kind of people they are. So, we might be told that support for people who are not working is 'holding out a temptation almost irresistible to become poor', or that any rational person who can receive benefits is going to choose not to work. The first of those was written in 1783,[22] the second in 1984.[23] Both are misconceived. Any choice that people make – if they have any choice – is shaped by the costs of receiving welfare, the things they are losing, the obstacles that they face, and the penalties they might have to undergo. The idea that people will choose not to work is easily disproved by looking at participation rates in the labour market, which are generally higher in countries with more provision.

The political discourse about welfare provision in Britain and America has reverted to the type of criticism that was made of the Poor Laws: that welfare locks people into poverty, that it breeds dependency, or that it leads to the formation of a shameless 'underclass', where one generation after another claims benefit. Most of this is groundless prejudice; none of it is true. The evidence that was supposed to prove that people were destined by genetics and biology to be poor or criminal was fabricated – made up by people who were so convinced it was true that cheating didn't really matter.[24] Ultimately this led to eugenics – the isolation and compulsory sterilization of 'defectives'[25] – and in due course to the Holocaust and mass murder.[26] The supposed persistence of poverty through 'intergenerational transmission' has been the subject of extensive research, but in richer economies it is hard to find; some researchers have compared it to the search for the Yeti.[27] The welfare state does not lock people into poverty: in developed countries, poverty is mainly transitory, most people get support at some time, and with the main exceptions of disability and old age, longer-term reliance on that support is relatively rare.[28] Children from disadvantaged families suffer proportionately more disadvantage, but in societies which are not poor, most do not grow up to be poor. The three main factors which account for this are education, partnering – poor people don't necessarily marry other poor people – and the state of the economy.[29] Poverty in contemporary economies is most commonly experienced at particular points in the life-cycle: childhood, young families, divorce, disability and old age. The welfare state is a response to these circumstances, not the cause of them. The more issues there are like this, the greater the welfare effort has to be.

That leaves us with the third set of objections, which is that welfare provision is unaffordable. That claim is based in part on the questionable assumption that the size of the cake is fixed, so that anything done by way of social provision is by definition a burden on the economy; another part is based in assumptions about the impact that social welfare provision might have on the productive economy. Neither position is consistent with the evidence.[30] As a broad generalization, richer countries spend more on public provision than poorer countries – that is part of the point of becoming richer. That general pattern means that the countries which might apparently be held back are the same ones that do best, and that means it is almost impossible to find any clear evidence that welfare actually hampers economic development. The studies which try to show that welfare is a bad thing can only do it by a sleight of hand, selecting particular countries at particular points in time (or worse, selecting different states in the USA, as if they were not part of the same polity or the same economy). There is no shortage of such studies, because the critics of the welfare state have been determined to prove their case, but they do not show what their authors think they do. As economist

Ronald Coase once said, if you torture the data long enough, it will confess.

The truth about all these contentions is that they don't really depend on evidence at all. The first group of arguments is about what governments should be permitted to do. The second set amounts to a claim that welfare has bad effects, when what the proponents really want to say is that it is bad for poor people to receive benefits and services that other people have paid for. And the third set of objections is not about whether the welfare state is affordable, but whether it should be afforded. These are moral positions, and if people are convinced of the rightness of their beliefs, whether or not the facts are there to back them up is probably the least important thing about them.

5

UNIVERSAL AND COMMUNITARIAN PERSPECTIVES

Any welfare state must face the question of inclusion. Who are the people that the services are intended for? The problem with any definition of rights based on citizenship – no matter how widely – is that sooner or later someone will be left out. Some people are deliberately excluded or socially rejected. It happens in many places that there will be stigmatization of people who are mentally ill, physically disabled or the victims of racism. Some of the people who are excluded are simply those who live outside the charmed circle: people who live in the wrong areas, members of the wrong ethnic or tribal group, and of course outsiders from abroad. This is from the Ypres report, published in 1531:

> We prefer our own citizens, whose persons and
> manners we know, to strangers with whom we have no
> acquaintance. We are duty bound to look after them,
> because they are members with us of one political body.
> We would be as ready to help anyone, but our resources
> are scarce enough to mean that we can help perfectly the
> need of our own poor folks: it is not enough to meet the
> needs of every man.[1]

Knowing who to provide for is one of the most basic challenges for any welfare system. This could have been written about almost any scheme in the last five hundred years.

This dilemma is often discussed under the unhelpful label of 'welfare chauvinism', a term that lumps together issues of citizenship, solidarity and social cohesion with racism and xenophobia. If we want to understand the moral basis for welfare in more depth, we need to express this issue in different terms. There is a powerful tension between *universalism* and *communitarianism*. Universalism applies common principles to everyone. Communitarianism argues that the principles which apply in different circumstances, and the structure of social obligations, can only be understood in the context of the society where they are applied.

Universalism

Many writers in social policy begin from a universalist position: they may not expect to include literally everyone, but they would want inclusion to be as broad and deep as possible. 'Human rights' are intrinsically universal, and principles like justice, equality or tolerance are commonly presented in universalist terms. Any moral principle that can be said to apply to everyone in the same circumstances is universal in this sense.

Even if there is an intention to cover the whole population, that can be done in many ways. Some services will be generally available; some will address broad categories of need such as disability or unemployment. Some will be residual, intended to cover issues that affect only small numbers: that is often the case with the protection of children from neglect or abuse. An aspiration to provide services for everyone does not necessarily translate into universal rights of citizenship.

The most basic argument for universalism is an argument for consistency – that people in the same circumstances should be treated in the same way. When we look at social policy in practice, however, universalism seems (perhaps unavoidably) to be subject to a series of compromises. In most cases, the provision of social welfare is tied to residence, citizenship or nationality. Benefits and services are not aimed at everyone, but at segments of a population – older people, children, minority groups such as indigenous peoples. The critical theorist Fiona Williams argues:

> The distrust of uniformity and universalism and the
> recognition of diversity and difference has emerged in two

ways within social policy. The first has been a 'top down' approach to diversity in the form of welfare pluralism. The second has been a 'bottom up' development of work around gender in particular, but also race, disability, age and sexuality. One consequence of this latter work has been to expose the 'false universalism' of the post war welfare state. ... Whilst welfare pluralism stresses the diversity of sources ... for welfare provision, the second places emphasis on the diversity of identity, experience, interest and need in welfare provision.[2]

If we had hoped to claim that the welfare state is truly there for everyone, we were always liable to be frustrated; there are unavoidable reservations, qualifications, limits and gaps in services. That does not invalidate the aspiration. The universalist principles associated with welfare states aim to achieve greater equality, material and personal security, social inclusion, the provision of services, and a recognition of general rights to welfare.

The social context

The principles that govern social policy depend on the social context where they are applied. They are socially constructed, because they have to be understood in terms of the relationships that make a society, and they are socially defined, taking on distinct meanings and applications in different settings. The principles are contingent, in the sense that their nature and force depend on the circumstances in which they are applied:

the political theorist Michael Walzer argues that 'All distributions are just or unjust relative to the social meanings of the goods at stake.'[3] They are contextual: they have to be applied in a specific social context, and lose some meaning when they are taken out of that context – fairness in the classroom is not the same thing as fairness in a court of law. And they are often particular: something that is true for people in one set of circumstances or relationships is not certain to be true for other people.

Principles which appear to be universal – such as 'Honour your father and mother' – still have to be refracted through the prism of social life; the rule implies a distinctive, personalized obligation for different people in different families. The United Nations Declaration of the Rights of the Child defines the human rights of children explicitly in those terms:

> The child, for the full and harmonious development of his personality, needs love and understanding. He shall, wherever possible, grow up in the care and under the responsibility of his parents, and in any case in an atmosphere of affection and of moral and material security. ...[4]

It is easy enough to see how this works between individuals – the obligations that we have for our own parents or children are not the same that we have for anyone else's. It can be more difficult to see how it applies to concepts such as poverty, disability, needs or welfare, but it does: these issues are no less socially constructed, contingent and dependent on the social context. Disability is widely interpreted in terms of a 'social model', describing the condition as a product of social construction.[5] Needs have to be translated from capabilities – we all need to have the capacity to do certain things, such as communication or mobility – into commodities, and the commodities which are used to achieve this are different in different societies.[6] Welfare is a broader term still, encompassing both resources and relationships at a personal, group or communal level; but the terms in which welfare is conceived are unavoidably defined and constructed in social terms.

The example of poverty brings many of these issues into relief. Most writers on poverty would accept that poverty is, to some extent, relative to the society where it occurs. That expression may, however, mean different things. For some writers, such as Martin Ravallion, formerly the Chief Economist for the World Bank, relative standards are standards that shift as lesser needs are satisfied: a relative standard of poverty is simply a more generous standard.[7] For others, relative poverty shows that poverty is socially defined: that social norms, decency and the understanding of what is 'essential' develop over time. For the sociologist Peter Townsend:

> People are relatively deprived if they cannot obtain, at all or sufficiently the conditions of life – that is, the diets, amenities, standards and services which allow them to play the roles, participate in the relationships and follow the

customary behaviour which is expected of them by virtue of their membership of society. If they lack or are denied the incomes. or more exactly the resources, including income and assets or goods or services in kind to obtain access to these conditions of life they can be defined to be in poverty.[8]

Others argue that poverty is socially constructed – that the items which it is possible to use, such as the definition of food or shelter, depend on the social context. Amartya Sen's concept of 'capabilities' suggests that while we all need to have the capacity to do certain things, such as communication or mobility, the commodities which are used to achieve this are different in different societies.[9]

These arguments share a crucial limitation: they are treating poverty as a state of being – a defined condition that people are in, or not in, that can be described at the level of the individual. There are forms and aspects of poverty that might be described in these terms: a lack of water, having no access to an energy supply. Economic analysis has tried to locate the response to poverty in terms of the condition of the individual, and much of what is presented as the 'measurement' of poverty is conceived in those terms. However, once we set foot beyond the confines of conventional academic discourse, expressions of poverty are not like that. When the World Bank conducted its major qualitative study, *Voices of the Poor*, it identified a range of issues that stretched across different societies.[10] Some of the themes are concerned with material circumstances; they include a concern with precarious livelihoods, problems of physical health and living in excluded locations.

> Health is number one because if you are ill you cannot work. (Zambia)

> I am going to be poor and even hungry if I cannot labour in the coming years due to old age. (Vietnam)

Other themes put more emphasis on social relationships: relationships of gender, social exclusion and lack of security.

> Where there is no security, there is no life. (Somaliland)

> Poverty is humiliation, the sense of being dependent on them, and of being forced to accept rudeness, insults, and indifference when we seek help. (Latvia)

And then there are political issues – limited communal organizations and abuse of authority by those in power.

> Poor people have no access to the police station, bank, government offices, and the judge of the village court. (Bangladesh)

> When the police come here, it is to rob us ... to humiliate everybody. (Brazil)

Poverty might be about money or things, but it might not be. It is described by poor people, around the world, as a set of issues concerned with relationships with other people. The many dimensions of poverty – inequality, economic distance, powerlessness, command over resources and exclusion – are not just socially constructed, and not just relative to the society where they occur. They are relational – made out of social relationships.[11] And that, in turn, tells us something important about the nature of social policy. Social policy involves rather more than an engagement with social relationships, but it is barely comprehensible without it.

Communitarianism

Communitarianism starts from a central focus on the relationships that people have with other people. It attempts to explain the pattern of rights and responsibilities as aspects of an interconnected social system. Our responsibilities are not responsibilities to everyone in the world: there are moral priorities, such as the priority one gives to members of one's own family or a local community. We are born into a series of networks, which begin with family life and go from there to make up a web of relationships and responsibilities. Moral and social obligations are necessarily located within a society, and an identifiable set of relationships; that also means that they differ (or at least, that they manifest themselves differently) for everyone. From a communitarian perspective, a statement of universal principles can never be enough: those principles have to be applied within specific social contexts, and different priorities can be attached to the various specific forms of implementation.[12]

Communitarianism locates each person in a set of networks that define a series of rights, obligations and social roles. Jeremy Seekings argues, from an African perspective, that there is a 'universalism of reciprocal obligation and community membership'; the influence of such ideas stands in contrast to the individualism that is so prominent in western liberal culture.[13] The fundamental glue of a society is solidarity: networks of social responsibility, where obligations and roles are intertwined. It is in the nature of solidarity that our obligations multiply and grow thicker in relation to the people we are closest to. The closest of these networks is usually a family, but the range of solidaristic networks, both formal and informal, is wide: it can be expressed through organizations, community, regional and national identity.

The very idea of a society refers to a complex system of overlapping, interlocked networks. In social terms, this is often translated into a concern with 'social cohesion'. Social cohesion can mean many things[14] – social ties, shared values, a sense of belonging, the ability to live and work together – but at root it must depend on the existence of relationships between different members of society. Part of this can be attributed to the relationships of family, religion and community, but there are limits to how effective or inclusive such factors can be. The idea of solidarity has been identified strongly with the principles of mutual support and 'gift-exchange' that were discussed in

Chapter 4, including altruism, balanced and generalized reciprocity. Reciprocity and mutuality are central to the development of enduring social obligations. The early advocates of solidarism – a political movement based on the concept of solidarity – emphasized the role of social insurance in social integration.[15] Over time, the emphasis has shifted towards broader forms of welfare provision.

This should help to explain something of the difficulties that surround questions of social inclusion. What obligations do people have to people who are not part of their society? This is not about 'chauvinism': it is about defining the limits of solidarity. If rights are tied strongly to social networks, they will exclude people who are marginal. If they are qualified or supplemented by principles of universal or human rights, the sorts of provision which follow are likely to be multi-tiered. Some people will have particular rights, such as earned pensions; others in society will have basic rights of citizenship; but outsiders will have only the human rights which are the minimum for everyone.

There are important reservations to make about communitarianism. It serves very well as a description of social relationships; it does much less well as a guide to moral action. Defining people as members of a group inevitably implies that some will be included, but others will not be. We know that our obligations to those who are closest to us are greater than those who are not so close; that is what being close means. But the model of social integration I have been discussing is intrinsically discriminatory. It has to be balanced with other, universalist principles – principles such as fairness, tolerance and empowerment. Without them, it can become exclusive, intolerant and unjust. Communitarianism needs, then, to be qualified – safeguarded by some universal rights – if it is to offer any protection for individuals or minorities.[16]

6

THE WELFARE STATE AND THE MARKET

Debates about the methods used in welfare states often focus on the relationship of public services to the 'market' – the complex series of production, distribution and exchange which is part of every economy. Some of the criticisms of welfare states reflect a view that social welfare services are inimical to the market – that markets make it possible for people to exercise choices, that the market should be able to arrange for the best possible allocation of resources, but that state-sponsored welfare diverts the flow of resources from how things ought to work. There is a tension here. It is all very well to argue that everything would be done better if things were left to private markets, but the same markets rely on people having money to spend, and ensuring that they have that money is another aspect of welfare provision.

The theory of how markets operate depends on the self-interest of producers, who provide goods and services for fee-paying customers. Adam Smith, the 18th-century professor who has some claim to be the founder of modern economic theory, famously made the case: 'It is not from the benevolence of the butcher, the brewer, or the baker, that we expect our dinner, but from their regard to their own interest.'[1] The ideal 'free market' is supposed to have multiple producers in competition with each other, free entry to and exit from the market, full information, no costs associated with location, and clear price signals. Nothing is perfect, of course, but the advocates of free markets generally argue that many important markets are close enough to that ideal, and that imperfect markets can usually be made better by guiding existing markets towards that model.

This view of the world is supported by some preposterous economic theory. The 'First Fundamental Theorem of Welfare Economics', so-called, claims that every competitive market equilibrium yields the most efficient allocation of resources.[2] As it stands, that claim is, pretty flatly, wrong. The conditions for it to apply are never met; real-world markets almost always offer compromises, and what is being looked for should be not the best possible allocation, but only one that is good enough. The test of efficiency that is used to justify the theoretical model ('Pareto optimality') states that the best outcome is one where at least one person is better off, and no one is worse off. The test is widely accepted by economists, but it is untenable – frankly, the sort of thing that gives economic theory a bad name. In economic terms, the demand for goods reflects people's relative purchasing power. In conditions of inequality, if only a few people are better off, others are going to be worse off, because they will be disadvantaged in any competition for scarce resources. A distribution where only a few people gain does not leave everyone else unaffected. That would only be true if the inequality has no effect on the prices that result or the distribution of goods; the assumption that this does not matter is inconsistent with basic economic principles.[3] In social terms, too, the theorem cannot cope with any problems that might stem from inequality,[4] or from people not having access to goods or services in the market. Philosopher Alan Ryan points out that the test could allow one person to have everything while others have nothing. He calls the standard 'intolerable' and 'repulsive'.[5] Pareto optimality is absurd, in both senses of the word – logically self-contradictory, and crackpot.

The Second Fundamental Theorem is supposed to show that markets can always be used, in conjunction with redistribution, to yield a desired result. 'On this basis', economic theorist Ross Starr writes, 'public authority intervention in the market through direct provision of services (housing, education, medical care, child care etc) is an unnecessary escape from market allocation mechanisms with their efficiency properties'.[6] There is a point buried in there, so long as we ignore the specific examples that Starr gives. There are some goods and services which can sensibly be distributed in the market. Most states in the world now give people cash support, so that they can buy things like food, fuel and clothing. The distribution of cash benefits, in preference to the direct provision of services, depends on there being a market to buy things from. Arguments for social protection, and for more 'radical' responses such as a universal basic income, generally accept that when poor people have access to money, they will spend it in a market.

Are things best left to the market in real life? The answer to that question is not straightforward – it depends on what kind of resource or service we are talking about. The case for distributing food through an economic market is fairly clear-cut. The distribution of food through shops has its deficiencies, but the main problems are a question of how much money people have to spend on food, not on whether there should be a National Food Service which might provide foodstuffs. (The idea is not completely wild: religious charity in Islam traditionally took the form of the distribution of bread, and after World War II, Britain had food rationing and control of the production of key foodstuffs like meat, milk and eggs.) Giving people money to spend works, more or less. One of the most persuasive reasons for the rapid expansion of cash benefits is pragmatic: cash (or at least, electronic credit) it is often the quickest and easiest way to get resources to people. It is also one of the most practical ways of developing and supporting markets in a formal economy.

Health care, by contrast, works rather badly in the market. The costs of medical care can be prohibitive, which is why private markets depend on insurance – pooled risks – rather than individual purchases. There is a profound gap between the information that is accessible to producers and consumers – that is, between doctors and patients. There are severe externalities – social consequences that are not necessarily taken into account in the transaction between doctor and patient. It is neither safe nor wise to leave people to their own devices if they have an infectious disease. There is good reason why almost all rich countries have developed non-market systems of health care. (The most visible exception to this is the USA – but even in the USA, millions of people are supported by federal or state programmes, such as the Veterans' Administration, Medicare or psychiatric care in state hospitals. The US system of health care is the most expensive in the world, and it leaves so many holes that government expenditure on health care in the USA still accounts for nearly a third of all its spending on health.)

The deficiencies in the market for health care are widely acknowledged. The same rationale has not, however, been generally applied to housing. The distribution of housing through the market is, for many people, erratic and inefficient.[7] Part of this relates to the pattern of land holding; in some societies, all the land is taken, while in others squatting on unclaimed land is the main option open to people who lack resources. Markets, when they apply, are highly localized, which gets in the way of full competition; the market only considers property that is vacant or being vacated, rather than the whole stock; prices are poorly related to production costs. Then there is the question of what can be traded – the sale and transfer of housing, or of tenancies, can only ever be for a very small part of the housing stock at a time. And there is nothing in the nature of a housing market which guarantees that people will be able to find something: a mismatch of provision and need, homelessness, overcrowding and people with no choice but to live in slums, are inherent in patterns of market provision. A United Nations report comments:

> In our world, one in eight people live in slums. In total, around a billion people live in slum conditions today. ... The impact of living in these areas is life threatening. Slums are marginalised, large agglomerations of dilapidated housing often located in the most hazardous urban land ... disengaged from broader urban systems and from the formal supply of basic infrastructure and services, including public space and green areas. Slum dwellers experience constant discrimination and disadvantage, lack of recognition by governance frameworks, limited access to land and property, tenure insecurity and the threat of eviction, precarious livelihoods, high exposure to disease and violence and, due to slums' location, high vulnerability to the adverse impacts of climate change and natural disasters.[8]

Given the importance of housing for human welfare and for public health, those problems really ought to imply a substantial set of non-market actions – but in many cases, and arguably most, they do not. Social housing is, admittedly, difficult to develop and deliver – but so is health care. That seems to point to some irrationality in the scheme of things. Much depends on what is conventional and what is accepted.

Market failures

Economists do accept that there are some situations which do not comfortably fit the model of the market. They call this 'market failure' – not, as a lay person might think, a case where a market has failed, but a set of special conditions which mean that markets cannot work in the way that the theory suggests. In principle, the operation of a free market in conditions of perfect competition should lead to optimal efficiency in the distribution of resources (though, as I have explained, the test which is being used to judge 'efficiency' is perverse, and should not be allowed to pass unchallenged). There are, however, cases where markets do not or cannot work as expected. Markets operate imperfectly when the assumptions do not apply: for example, where there are costs associated with location, where there is insufficient competition, where there is not free entry to or exit from the market by suppliers, or where information is incomplete. 'Market failure', however, arises not just in circumstances where the conditions of a perfect market do not apply (because they never do in an ideal form), but in cases where they cannot conceivably apply. This may be specialized, but, Joseph Stiglitz argues, the problems are pervasive and hard to ignore.[9]

The classic example of market failure is the case of 'social goods'. These are goods, like public parks, which are not divisible, which are not exclusive, and not consumed by individuals. Clean air is an easy example. It is non-rivalrous – the open air does not diminish in quality or quantity because other people breathe it. It is non-excludable – it is not really possible to stop other people from using it. The benefits of street lighting, storm drains and public roads are not quite perfect examples, but they are close enough.

Some other examples of 'market failure' reflect conditions which make it impossible to rely wholly on competitive production and exchange. There are commodities and services, like those in medical care, where there is an imbalance in power between the producer and the consumer, and where the consumer's ability to choose may be constrained. People cannot be expected to 'shop around' to get treatment for their cancer. There are 'natural' monopolies, which make it difficult to allow markets to operate effectively – it makes no sense for five suppliers all to offer piped water to the same street. There may be externalities, that is, effects which are experienced by people who are not parties to the commercial transaction. Negative externalities include issues like pollution, which is usually the by-product of someone else's economic choices, or climate change. Positive externalities include the benefits of public health programmes, such as vaccinations, which also reduce the risk of people who are not vaccinated, and of education in schools, which means that future employers get the benefits of a trained population. Understanding the 'market' solely in terms of individual transactions distorts preferences by not taking such implications into account. In each of these cases – constrained choice, natural monopolies or externalities – advocates of market-based provision have tried to get around the problems by creating the conditions for a market in some respects (competitive health insurance, 'choices' between agencies that bill for services, and charging polluters) while leaving other non-market elements in place.

Economists often identify market failure as the best justification for public action. It is not, even if it is an important one. The problem is that markets – even the best, most effective markets – depend on people having the money to participate in them. The advocates of markets are keen on saying that markets offer consumers a choice. That is only half the story. Free markets also offer a choice to producers. Producers do not have to supply goods to the people who are poor or difficult to help. It follows: markets leave gaps. This is not 'market failure'; it is what markets are supposed to do.

Real-world economics

Market theory is highly idealized, both in how it works and what it can achieve. The term 'neoliberal' describes the political ideology of people who want that theory to be followed as fully as possible.[10] That approach depends, necessarily, on an heroic oversimplification of how the economy works.[11]

The way that social welfare provision generally works in practice is not much like commercial production. The first difference is about profit. Many of the organizations engaged in the provision of social welfare are non-profit-making. Voluntary societies, religious foundations (such as waqfs), charities and trades unions have played a major part in the development of social welfare provision. Being not-for-profit does not mean that they do not use money, but at root they are not there either to compete with rivals or to maximize their returns; if returns are larger than necessary, the main option that a non-profit organization has is to extend its activities. There may be selfish interests that drive people who are working for non-profit-making agencies, but they are more likely to be about long-term security or personal career advancement than about maximizing financial returns.

If we are looking for hospitals, schools and charitable foundations to fit the pattern of the firms that appear in economics textbooks, we are going to be disappointed. Even within profit-making concerns, there may be other considerations besides profit. There are social enterprises, set up to meet perceived needs, and elements of corporate social responsibility, which whatever its limitations does allow people engaged in profit making to engage with broader social objectives. (This has always been part of market-based activity. The anthropologist David Graeber points out that Adam Smith's butchers and bakers didn't just work for profit. In the economy of the day, they had to cultivate goodwill, and goodwill meant that they had to extend trust and credit – often to rich and poor alike.[12])

The second difference stems from a different interpretation of self-interest. In the sort of crude economic theory favoured by neoliberals, everyone is out for themselves, and they will be guided principally by the gains or losses they might make as individuals. Economic theory offers us a picture of a world where firms are independent, rational, self-interested and aiming to make the maximum amount of profit. This is not much like the world we live in. Firms will balance short-term profit with long-term interests, the management of risks and vulnerabilities, and a sense of whether the payment is reasonable. Producers commonly set prices, not on the basis of maximizing profits, but of finding a price that is considered fair.[13]

Mutual aid can quite sensibly be thought of as another expression of self-interest. The trades union movements of the 19th and 20th centuries referred, not infrequently, to fraternity, solidarity, internationalism and the 'brotherhood of man'. In the main, however, people join mutual aid societies, not because their hearts are brimming with unbridled altruism, but because it is a very practical way of managing risk and reducing vulnerability. In Britain, the building societies made it possible for people to buy houses by pooling the financial resources of their members. Some building societies disappeared over time, because they were only ever intended to be temporary; the permanent building societies went on to become a major pillar of the banking system. Mutual insurance companies became part of the foundations of the financial system. There has been a trend to 'de-mutualization' in some fields, when members have realized that the pooled resources have a capital value that greatly exceeds the potential benefits – this has happened to building societies, banks and insurers – but that is only possible because the resources were pooled in the first place. Under current pressures, there has been a revival of mutual insurance in some places, often in small, tightly defined organizations. In their nature, the coverage that such organizations can offer is too restrictive to be universal.[14]

Government is not central to these systems, but governments have had to decide what they are going to do in circumstances where non-profits and mutual aid play a prominent role. There are circumstances where governments have decided to supplement the work of such agencies, and to fill in the gaps – that has been the approach of the USA to health care, or of France to social security. In some countries, governments have aimed to take over: that was what the British government did to the mutualist 'friendly societies'. Governments might compel people who are not included to participate – the position in Scandinavian countries relating to social insurance. Alternatively, they may push mutuals and non-profits into the commercial sector, which has been done to a series of building societies and banks in the UK.

Governments and the market

Critics of government activity often begin from a position where markets have already developed, and governments 'intervene' in the natural order of things. State intervention – tampering with things that matter to people, and governing their actions – is an unacceptable intrusion into people's lives. This is a distortion of perspective. Markets have developed, after all, in conditions where the actions of the state have defined what is and what is not possible: a framework of law, various regulations, patterns of enforcement and adjudication, and so on. In many societies, and in particular in the most developed economies, the role of government stretches some way beyond that: growth and development have typically taken place with subsidies, incentives, investment and employment negotiated with governments.[15]

Markets do not necessarily achieve their results spontaneously. The operation of commercial transactions depends heavily on the establishment of a common legal and regulatory framework – that has been done by governments throughout recorded history. However, governments may well have to make decisions on a different basis from the way that production and allocation are settled in commercial transactions. Some contemporary commentators are sceptical about that. They accuse governments of imposing their own values on others – spending money on 'merit goods', that is, things which are thought to be morally desirable – and of doing things less effectively than markets do. According to the critics, governments fail when political processes interfere with economic mechanisms;[16] when politics leads to negotiation, bargaining and compromise;[17] and when the government choices are not the efficient outcomes that are produced by markets. All that adds up to a complaint that governments don't do things the way that commercial markets do. The obvious answer to that is: yes, that's the point. Markets represent the cumulative actions of many individuals, forming preferences and choices independently. Governments may legitimately want to do something different from markets.

In some circumstances, governments may aim to change the conduct of individuals. They may need to regulate the conduct of some in order to protect others – for example, in controlling the supply of drugs, or taking action about pollution. And governments may not be prepared to accept the consequences of individual decisions. The management of risk is changed when numbers are large. A risk of 1 in 10,000 is remote; it makes perfect sense for an individual, given a choice in preparing for the contingency, to dismiss it. In a country with 50 million inhabitants, that apparently trivial risk will affect 5,000 people. We saw a similar effect very plainly during the COVID-19 pandemic, when a cabal of neoliberal commentators could not understand why governments were not ready to let the disease spread. From the perspective of individuals, they argued, people will take their chances. From the perspective of government, that approach would have been intolerable.

At times, too, the choices and decisions that governments are called on to make are not about individuals as such. They may need to take into account the interests of large groups: a demographic category (such as 'children' or 'older people'), an industrial sector, a territory, a society. There are important aspects of social life that markets largely fail to touch. Issues such as the socialization of children, social order, international relations or defence may well come into play. Government action has to consider other criteria.

7

SOME CHALLENGES FOR THE WELFARE STATES

The challenges faced by welfare states are considerable. Some of those challenges are inherent in the nature of the exercise – they are what you might expect from taking on any major project. Delivering services to whole populations is never going to be simple or cheap. In the early 1990s, the World Bank and the World Health Organization set out the case for Basic Health Care Packages. The aim was to cover a set of health measures which could use limited resources to the best effect.[1] The initial programmes were limited and austere. They focused on such issues as maternity care and the prevention of transmissible disease; deliberately, they excluded more expensive patterns of treatment, such as psychiatric care or support for older people. As this approach has been extended to other countries with lower incomes or lower middle incomes, the range of services that might be included has extended. There has been a considerable stress, too, on engagement and partnership, giving more people a voice in the development of health care.[2]

Size

The first, and in some ways the most obvious, of the challenges facing the welfare state is that welfare states are big. That word, 'big', is relative: whatever the size of the country may be, the aspirations associated with welfare states call for services to have a mass role. Providing a service for a million people is not much like providing a service for twenty. In principle, a service for twenty people can be personal, individuated, responsive and sensitive. A service for a million people has to be planned rather differently: it calls for organization, identification of tasks, divisions of labour, consideration of resources and much else besides.

Many governments have tried to reduce the size of the task by 'targeting' services. If governments and other providers are able to select what they do and who they do it for, they may be able to limit what they do, and hold the pressures in line. In practice, however, targeted benefits and services tend to work rather badly. It is often difficult to identify who is poor or who is most in need, and the more a government is trying to do, the more difficult it becomes. Targeted services often do not get to the people they are supposed to get to – there is always a problem of 'takeup'. People do not necessarily know about the service, they may not think it is available to them and, because the tests and assessments are burdensome to comply with, they may not be ready or able to make the effort to claim. The tests create major problems of equity at the boundaries, the points at which people may or may not be entitled to claim. It can seem arbitrary as to who qualifies, and who does not;[3] and it is difficult, once a link to a service has been established, to decide when the service should be withdrawn.[4] A report for Development Pathways has attempted to identify how effective different methods of targeting are in getting money to the poor in 30 low- and middle-income countries. The best performing programme targeted on the poor, in Brazil, relied on a test of income and failed to reach 44% of the eligible group. The worst performing, in Rwanda, used community based targeting, and left out more than 97% of the intended recipients.[5]

Service delivery

The problems of service delivery are rather different according to the nature of the service provided. Consider, on one hand, the delivery of services in person – services like medical care, schooling or the care of older people. It is basic to those services that the person receiving the service has to be there physically. It is no less basic that the recipient consequently plays some part in the process. This relationship has been called 'co-production': it takes two to tango.[6] The service needs to be where the people are. Either the service must come to the people, or the people must come to the service.

It follows that preparing human services for a mass role has to be planned and organized geographically. That will usually call for a physical infrastructure – hospitals, clinics, schoolrooms, transport links – as well as basic items that are called for whenever people congregate, such as sanitation, food and water. The 'Big Bang' in Uganda offers an extreme illustration. The government of Uganda wanted to ensure that every child – or at least, the vast majority of children – should have access to elementary education, and aimed to do it all at once. Between 1997 and 2003, the numbers of children being educated went from 2.7 million to 7.3 million.[7] Finding physical places urgently for four-and-a-half million children is staggeringly difficult. Who will teach them? Where can they sit? What about books, pencils, paper? Where can they have a drink of water? Where can they go the toilet? The World Bank, reviewing Big Bang schemes in Uganda, Kenya, Ethiopia and Malawi, was sceptical: there were major problems with class sizes and finding resources.[8] The answer, however, is not to avoid doing it; it is to try to do it better.

Then consider the delivery of cash assistance, which works in other ways entirely. Increasingly, the distribution of cash resources is being done through electronic credits. The need to make contact directly with the recipient has not gone away altogether, because there will still be checks to run, but the distribution of cash is not personalized in the same way as physical care. Cash offers the means to buy commodities; there may well be moneylenders who treat cash as just another commodity, but social assistance or social insurance have to be delivered on different principles.

The relative ease of cash payment, and the simplicity of the institutional structure, is a major reason why cash assistance has been adopted by so many countries. Having said that, it should not be imagined that distributing money to people is straightforward. The task begins with identification of the intended population, possibly with some sort of publicity and public information. Usually it requires some sort of documentation. Then there is verification, assessment of eligibility, decisions about the method of distribution and delivery.[9] An issuing authority will need to have rules in place about assignment (whether someone else, such as a creditor, can take over the payment) and termination (what happens, for example, when someone dies?). There is a large, and generally rather naive, literature advocating a universal basic income for everyone.[10] That would have the great advantage of avoiding complicated tests of income or special need. However, there is much more than that to delivering cash benefits, and the literature to date hasn't acknowledged or tried to engage with most of the practical problems.[11]

Information management

A third set of issues relate to information management. Some services can be delivered to all comers, despite knowing little or nothing about the recipients – that is true of disaster relief, soup kitchens or hospital clinics – but for other services, such as cash assistance, schools or housing provision, it is hard, and sometimes impossible, to deliver services effectively without having a record of what is done and who it is done for. In some countries, people do not have identity papers or ways of showing that they exist, such as a birth certificate; in some countries, they do not even have physical addresses. The situation is changing rapidly, as governments roll out schemes that require people to have identity papers. Modern technology has certainly helped; examples are the use of the Global Positioning System in countries where many people have no physical address, and the introduction in India of the Aadhar card, which serves both as identity and a link to social welfare. The development of new technology, however, is not a panacea, and often there are major gaps left.

It has been a general experience that attempts to 'target' individual needs rarely live up to expectations. Some things about a person are reasonably constant and predictable, even if there are occasional exceptions: their name, their age, their gender and, for pensioners, their work record. Some things change more rapidly: addresses, relationships, the composition of their household. But some things change from day to day or week to week, including physical capacity (many people with disabilities say they are disabled 'sometimes') and, most changeable of all, income. Governments might want to target income and physical capacity, but few governments have the ability to track and use that information reliably. Working as an adviser, I have tried to tell politicians that claimants often don't know, not just what their income is, but whether they are disabled, whether they are in a stable personal relationship or if they are employed. Usually my argument is met with a look of bafflement or disbelief. The politicians' incomprehension is reflected in processes that expect people to report their situation accurately, and threaten them with criminal prosecution if they do not. More than fifty years ago, Richard Titmuss trenchantly criticized 'computermania': the conviction that if only we could devise a master computer programme to run the system, all our troubles would be over. Computers, he objected, cannot supply answers to the sort of human problems which lie under these processes.[12] That is as true now as it was then.

Resources: paying for welfare

There are several different types of expenditure which a welfare state ought to provide for. They include funding for a social infrastructure, including both capital projects and training and maintaining a professional workforce. There will be labour costs associated with public employment. There will be the costs of services that are sub-contracted or purchased. And there will be the cost of goods obtained for the delivery of services: public housing does not come cheap. However, many countries abandoned this way of accounting for expenditure in the 1960s and 1970s, with the development of programme budgeting; it is more common now to find a stated bill for health, housing, social security and so on.

Public sector accounts are largely set as a matter of convention, rarely taking full account of the contribution of public services.[13] The conventions have a powerful influence, but they are only one way of looking at the issue. There is a general assumption that the 'welfare state' is part of the state: some is, and some isn't. There is a tendency to disregard private sector expenditure and borrowing in key areas of welfare provision, such as health care or education. Some transactions are diverted to be 'off-book', a pretence that they are not actually part of the finance of welfare provision. Transfer payments are routinely, and misleadingly, classified as public spending. If governments were to agree to account differently for transfer payments, social investment or production, the apparent costs of welfare state provision would change, too.

I am used to the way that things are done in the UK, where the main pillars of the welfare state are treated as public expenditure. In France, the conventions that applied for most of the post-war period were constructed on different terms altogether. Things are done differently now, but in the 1990s, the focus of political interest was whether key funds were in surplus or in deficit, not what the total expenditure was. The protests against government plans to close *le trou de la Sécu* – the 'hole in Social Security', actually a deficit in health care funding – marked a clash between two quite different ways of understanding what sort of problem the hole was. (There were demonstrations in the streets protesting plans for a national health service. Left-wing organizations such as Force Ouvrière feared that the proposal would undermine existing provision.) It is not a simple matter, then, of lining up one country against another to see who spends more. What matters is how and where the money is used.

How do welfare states raise the money? One of the great myths in this field is that it must mean higher taxes. The finance of state activity can be managed through tax, but there are other methods. They include contributions (many welfare systems are non-governmental; some are voluntary); conscripted labour, which is the basis of national defence in many countries; other voluntary payments (such as lotteries or donations); nationalization and sequestration (governments can, and do, claim or confiscate resources); charges; government commerce (for example, profits on government enterprise), and other revenue (such as returns on investment, or the acquisition, development and sale of resources. Iran's welfare system is largely funded through the sale of oil). A tax system, meanwhile, serves other purposes besides paying for welfare. Those purposes include raising revenue for public functions; repricing, intended to change the way market signals work (for example, taxes on tobacco); redistribution; changing behaviour (incentives, disincentives and subsidies); conveying a moral position (such as support for families or religious charities); fiscal policy, using tax measures to steer an economy; and extending solidarity, by recognizing rights and imposing responsibilities. Raising resources, then, is not a simple, straightforward exercise, any more than choosing which services to develop is simple. It involves, like all policy decisions in this field, a mish-mash of competing, often conflicting, aims and methods.

This is not the end

To read some of the criticisms directed at the modern 'welfare state', one might imagine that the exercise has been a total failure. On the political right, there are the neoliberals, who see the whole thing as a drain on the economy and an imposition on people's personal freedom. They argue, straightforwardly enough, that markets are simply the best method of production and distribution available to humanity – that argument was addressed in the previous chapter. Neoliberals consider that property is the most fundamental right we have and that all redistribution is a violation of that right. There are two key objections to that. One is that such rights are not absolute: every measure to protect the weak from the strong redistributes rights, and laws redistribute freedoms. The other lies in a central misunderstanding, that social welfare provision is all based on coercion. Redistribution in many cases, if not most, is voluntary – it is implicit in the mutual aid and insurance schemes that people sign up to. The liberals of the 19th century, such as JS Mill and Dicey, understood this; contemporary neoliberals, following the likes of von Mises and Rothbard, don't.

Marxists, at the other end of the political spectrum, argue that the welfare state is essentially a compromise with capitalism, locked in a permanent state of crisis because the demands it makes of the economy are incompatible with the pursuit of private profit. The best the welfare state can do in such circumstances is to put a sticking plaster on things – as David Garland puts it, producing a set of systems and institutions designed to manage problems rather than to deal with them.[14] There are different schools of Marxist thought, but they have mainly leaned to the view that social rules serve the interests of a dominant class and that social welfare services have been won by organized labour in the teeth of opposition from that class. There are some historical developments that can be read that way, but the relationship between governments and organized labour have been much less conflictual; in much of western Europe, unions have been treated as 'social partners', contributing to political negotiations and in some cases providing and managing services themselves.[15] Former President Barack Obama comments about the USA: 'It was the labor movement that helped secure so much of what we take for granted today. The 40-hour work week, the minimum wage, family leave, health insurance, Social Security, Medicare, retirement plans. The cornerstones of the middle-class security all bear the union label.'[16]

We cannot assume that every aspect of social welfare services is devoted to the service of a capitalist economy. Which part of a welfare state, we might well ask, is not going to be needed after the demise of capitalism? Are there going to be no doctors and no hospitals, because no one will be sick? No schools, because everyone will be born with the ability to read and write? No pensions, because goods will be exchanged without money? No one should imagine that welfare states are perfect, but that is a long way from supposing that they are defined by their place in a capitalist system.

There is some common ground between the Marxists of the left and the neoliberals of the right. Both suppose that the welfare state cannot be reconciled with the process of private economic production. They are equally misguided. It may happen that some social policies will divert resources that would otherwise be expended on private activity. That is a long way, however, from a claim that the public and private production are incompatible. Supporting children and older people, which is the bulk of what welfare states actually do, can hardly be supposed to cause serious damage to the structure of an economy. When it comes to the labour force, which is the focus of much of the concern that critics express, there is little substance to the charge: richer countries which have better facilities also tend to have higher labour market participation.[17] In practice, countries with more generous provision have been better able to grow economically than places which have not had equivalent protections. Services such as health care or education strengthen an economy. Cash benefits help to regulate economic activity and maintain demand in markets which could not otherwise function. Creating a physical infrastructure for energy, transport and communications generally works in favour of productive enterprise. The economist Ha-Joon Chang argues that a well-designed welfare system can make national economies more flexible, adaptable and dynamic.[18]

A recent book on European welfare states comments:

> contemporary politicians, academics, and other observers have (whether gleefully or mournfully) been predicting the end of the welfare state since at least the 1970s. Half a century on, the welfare state is still around. Indeed, it is in rude health, if the share of national income going to social protection – higher than ever – is any indication. How can so many people, including first-class scholars, have got it so wrong?[19]

Many of the critics of welfare services are convinced that welfare states are trying to do the wrong things, in the wrong way, and they have argued for things to be done differently. The problem with those criticisms is not that they are wrong in every conceivable case, but that they hardly touch the surface of what is actually happening. In the course of this short book, I have been emphasizing the diversity of aims, institutions and methods that characterize welfare states around the world. That diversity lies not just between different regimes, but within them. Anyone who imagines that there must be one fundamental explanation underlying all this hasn't grasped what's going on.

8

THE WELFARE STATES: PAST, PRESENT AND FUTURE

Studies of the welfare state have mainly focused on the richer countries. That is not surprising: those are the countries which have developed their systems of support first and most fully, providing examples to countries that have only engaged with welfare provision more recently. That has been true even for countries in Europe: the systems of southern European countries, such as Spain and Italy, have been classified as 'rudimentary'.[1]

The dominant narratives have come from Germany and Britain. Germany, a state founded only in 1871, developed under Bismarck a national system of social insurance, based on contributions made during employment, and covering sickness, industrial injuries and pensions. That system survived through Nazism and two world wars. After 1945, the government built on those foundations to develop a *Sozialstaat* or 'social state', perhaps better understood as a 'social market economy'. Social welfare was co-opted in the cause of economic development: the system depended heavily on a person's work record, with some gaps for the better-off (deemed not to need support) and the poorest (who had not contributed).

The German system became the exemplar of two conflicting accounts of the 'welfare state'. On one hand, it made the case for seeing welfare as a means to support the capitalist economy. On the other, it fuelled a view of welfare as a field of conflict between capital and labour, where any concessions won by the labour movement were liable to be subverted by a rigged system. Subsequently, Marxist writers came to argue that there was an unresolvable tension between welfare systems and the interests of capital. 'While capitalism cannot exist with, nor can it exist without, the welfare state.'[2] The German system stands as testimony that this is simply not true; the two systems have relatively little difficulty in operating side-by-side.

The British narrative begins with the Poor Law. The Poor Law was a comprehensive, national provision for those who were destitute; it became the foundation of a wide range of other services, including health, education and local government, simply because there was no other authority in place that could provide them. The creation of the welfare state in 1948 was heralded as a fundamental break with the past: supposedly, services of a new and different kind. This narrative has been powerfully persuasive: its influence can be seen in accounts of services in countries, such as the USA and Australia, which did not have the Poor Law. Wilensky and Lebeaux, two American writers, memorably described this as a move from residual to 'institutional' welfare.[3] In a residual model of welfare, welfare is only a safety net, called on when other ways of dealing with issues are not available. The institutional model of welfare goes well beyond a safety net: it treats a range of contingencies, such as sickness, unemployment and old age, as a normal part of social life, and offers a standard set of responses to such conditions. The implication is that welfare states develop through a movement from safety nets to more extensive systems.

There are three narratives here: the residual model, the social market economy and the institutional model. They were first identified by Richard Titmuss, at that time the leading scholar in the study of social policy.[4] Subsequently, Titmuss' models were adapted by Gøsta Esping-Andersen to represent the 'welfare regimes'. The residual model became 'liberal' – a category that included Britain. The social market economy became 'corporatist'. Institutional welfare became 'social democratic'.[5] The structures of Swedish social policy may have reflected the corporatist approach,[6] but Swedish policies advocated solidarity, equality and democracy, and that made Sweden a better fit for the model of institutional welfare than Britain was.[7]

These terms effectively generalized from the historical narratives, translating them into a theoretical framework. In that framework, the development of welfare services seems to suggest a progressive movement between ideal types: from residual to institutional welfare, from laissez-faire markets to decommodified state provision, from insecurity to social protection,[8] or from liberalism to social democracy, possibly moving towards socialism.[9] It is possible to see welfare in these terms, but in its nature the evidence is selective – it has to be. Esping-Andersen argues that his classification is based on 'the principles embedded in the welfare state', represented by rights, the balance of state and market provision, and 'stratification', which includes (among other factors) corporatism, poor relief and the coexistence of private systems.[10] His approach depends, in large part, on finding some way to use the available data to reflect the normative issues he wants to highlight. The same is true of all the imitators and rivals who want to modify the analysis; selective data have to be available and matched to the model. There are always likely to be disputes about the accuracy and reliability of such figures, but the problem here is not really about finding better ways to measure things; there will always be a host of other factors and other services that might have been included instead. The best one can hope for is to find some persuasive indicators or pointers that can help, in conjunction with other indicators, to sum up the points at issue, and that is what Esping-Andersen has done.

I have already remarked on the problems that result from this kind of approach: the misclassifications, the black swans, the details that are overlooked or overridden. Core principles have not been considered, such as the British stress on uniform coverage, the German emphasis on subsidiarity (which reserves power to more local organizations), or the strongly communitarian elements of the Swedish 'people's home'. Many services have not been referred to directly – for example, education, disability, housing or social care. The diverse arrangements have been reduced to the briefest of outlines.

The more detail that is provided, the less adequate those outline accounts seem to be. Lutz Leisering has guided a series of cross-national studies, looking at the development of welfare in a range of countries – among them China, Brazil, India and South Africa.[11] The main effect of close historical investigation is to undermine any broad generalizations one might wish to make about the development and structure of social welfare services. Some of the measures taken will reflect common influences (such as the conventions of the International Labour Organization, or the terms set by the World Bank), and there may be some imitation of neighbouring countries (as there has been in Latin America), but these do not add up to the adoption of consistent welfare regimes. At best, there is only a 'family resemblance' between aspects of different services in different countries. That should not completely invalidate any generalizations one might wish to make, but it does call for caution. We are never going to understand the development of welfare around the world if we persist in focusing on a small handful of rich countries. We need to break away from the conventions of regime analysis that have occupied scholars for the last thirty years.

An alternative narrative

The starting point for an alternative narrative is indeterminate, for a simple reason: there isn't one. In a vast range of societies, there have been arrangements to deal with people when they had problems, or posed them, or when they were poor and needed support.[12] From the earliest times, there have been attempts to formalize such arrangements: we can see this, for example, in the biblical instructions about how to help the poor, how to manage debts, when to share and where the limits of responsibility lay. Religious charity was the most salient method of service delivery, but it was not the whole story; there were trusts and foundations, and the mutual aid societies established by the guilds. In Europe, the Church sought and established control of much of this effort in the 9th century, criticizing the abuses it had witnessed in private foundations; six hundred years later, reformers levelled many of the same accusations against the Church, and sought the intervention of the civic authorities.

Over time, the scope of these arrangements has tended to expand. Some of the arrangements will be made through institutions such as churches and mosques; some through supplementary measures, such as the common funds (or 'community chests') developed in Lutheran communities; some through trades unions and mutual aid; some through commercial activity. There is another, less familiar, set of developments: the growth of 'clandestine' or outlaw welfare provision, made by criminal gangs, drug cartels, terrorists, rebel militias and the like. Some of the services provided by criminal activity are 'involuntary', such as employment, but much is based in direct provision – and engagement with these services may be backed up by physical force.[13] None of these is likely to be comprehensive – they all include some people, and exclude or fail to include others.

The early efforts of government might have aimed to fill the gaps, but it is just as likely that those efforts too will have been piecemeal. Many contemporary governments aim to satisfy particular constituencies – perhaps their own supporters, perhaps specific tribes or ethnic groups. Clientelism – distributing benefits as favours, and favouring some groups over others – is rife. However, once a government has accepted even a partial role in the provision of welfare services, it will find that the pressure to extend the scope of the service increases, and that there are political and economic advantages in doing so.

The many schemes that have been developed round the world are not untypically dependent on location – for example, where health care is based physically in a hospital. Some schemes focus on poorer areas; some are confined to specific areas for practical reasons, such as policies that are confined to the cities. (Urban areas tend to be better protected than rural ones.) Some are implemented by local and regional governments rather than nationally. The process of expansion tends to be incremental, as more arrangements are made and added to the welfare mix. That is not the same as saying that things develop gradually – they are far more likely to develop in fits and starts. They have grown through a process that political scientists call 'punctuated equilibrium': nothing seems to change, but then there is a sudden flurry of measures.

The next stage in development, beyond partial, piecemeal provision and clientelism, is the extension of solidarity. This is an attempt, in principle, to expand the range and scope of measures to ensure that much larger numbers of people have some sort of protection. There may be a more general motivation behind it – it is part of Catholic social teaching – but in practice, it suggests a patchwork quilt of overlapping arrangements, often with a few holes left in it. Social insurance, arguably the main method of doing this, is used extensively for pensions and for health care. It is in the nature of insurance, however, that people are expected to make some sort of contribution to the scheme before they can withdraw any benefit. The Beveridge scheme in the UK claimed to be covering people universally, 'from the cradle to the grave', but there were marked gaps in the system – such as provision for housing costs, or protection of lone parents. Many people were left out, and the residual, safety scheme of National Assistance came to play a 'mass role'. The French *régime général* brought in workers who were not covered otherwise, but by the 1970s, when all workers were included, there were still millions of people who were not protected. Solidarity, in its nature, falls somewhat short of comprehensive provision. Many of the best-known comprehensive schemes turn out not to be comprehensive at all.

As solidarity continues to expand, it becomes impossible to draw a clear line between that process and the aspirations of a welfare state. Even as it is hardly possible to identify a clear start to the process, so it is hard to define any threshold or finishing point that would tell us that the work is finished.

In the same way, as more people engage in relationships of solidarity, it comes nearer and nearer to a principle of universality – the claim to cover everyone. Even if the provision is not universal, it is not uncommon for governments to justify what they do in universalist terms. The Universal Declaration of Human Rights states, among many other themes, that:

> Everyone, as a member of society, has the right to social security and is entitled to realization, through national effort and international co-operation and in accordance with the organization and resources of each State, of the economic, social and cultural rights indispensable for his dignity and the free development of his personality.[14]

The way in which this is expressed allows a considerable latitude in the interpretation and implementation of the principle: it all depends on which country is being considered. That argument is consistent with communitarianism. Communitarian policies, in their nature, fall short of universal treatment. In every welfare state, there are major limitations on who – that is, which people – will be served.

Figure 1 shows the development of welfare states in schematic terms. It only offers a patchwork, not a design for the welfare state. There is no certainty that everything will follow on in the same way.

Figure 1: How welfare states develop

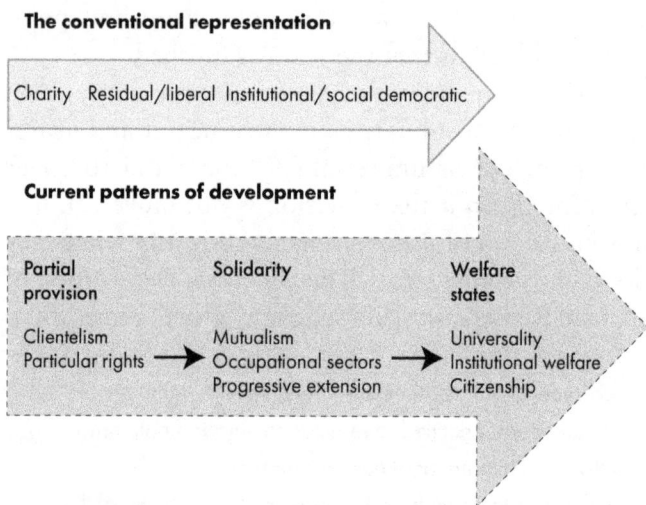

The conventional representation

Charity   Residual/liberal   Institutional/social democratic

Current patterns of development

Partial provision	Solidarity	Welfare states
Clientelism Particular rights →	Mutualism Occupational sectors Progressive extension →	Universality Institutional welfare Citizenship

Current trends

Where, we might well ask, is this heading? Social science is much better at analysing past and present than predicting the future. There are, I think, three trends which are particularly noteworthy.

The first is the growth of democratic norms, and the changing patterns of governance associated with them. This is visible in the acceptance of the legitimacy of electoral processes, the influence of the media, the establishment of partnership working in national plans, and the recognition that governments have to engage and work with other actors. In relation to electoral processes, it has long been observed that many elections are rigged: referenda are a tool beloved of demagogues. Why, then, do governments do it? Hypocrisy, the saying has it, is the homage that vice pays to virtue. They do it because they think it makes them look good, and they are probably right to think so. That position is reinforced by the exchange of social benefits and public employment for political support – the 'authoritarian support coalitions' described by Eibl.

The influence of the media is less certain, but Amartya Sen has made the case that the critical role of independent media has been central to poverty reduction. In his view, quite simply, the media make it more difficult for governments to do bad things, or to ignore the most blatant forms of corruption.[15] (This position is probably reinforced by another trend, which has little to do with formal institutions: that is the widespread use of modern cell phones in poor countries, especially in Africa.[16])

The development of social planning reflects the influence of international organizations.[17] The European Union requires it of all its members, and asks governments that receive aid from it to form strategies: currently the European Union, the largest donor to sub-Saharan Africa, is in the process of developing a 'Strategy for Africa'. 67 low-income countries have gone through the process of preparing the Poverty Reduction Strategies demanded by the International Monetary Fund and the World Bank,[18] and aid to middle-income countries effectively takes the numbers over 100. While other general conditions about governance may or may not be effective, a Swiss team focusing on development studies argues that the difference has been made by requirements to engage partners from civil society; the effect has been to make governments less able to divert funds to their own use, and more sensitive to public priorities.[19]

The second trend has been the explosion of interest in social policy, from governments around the world. This is visible in the development of national schemes for health care, education and social protection. We can see the positive impacts clearly in certain social indicators. Child mortality – one of the strongest pointers to the health of mothers, as well as the health of children – has fallen dramatically around the world. Since 1990, it has fallen worldwide by more than half (93 deaths per 1,000 to 38 per 1,000 in 2021); in the least developed countries, it has fallen by nearly two-thirds (176 per 1,000 to 61).[20]

The third trend is movement in the opposite direction: the trend to retrenchment. This has been called 'austerity'. Austerity used to mean the provision of services at only the most basic level, stripped down to a minimum.[21] The term has been hijacked to imply something rather different: austerity has been described as 'a means of reducing the size and economic role of the state, particularly with respect to social welfare provision'.[22] Reducing the size of the state is not at all the same thing as cutting costs. 'Austerity' policies commonly shift the burden of responsibility from public expenditure to private citizens, and that is liable to cost more overall, especially when austerity is coupled with the priorities of profit-making firms, the duplication of services inherent in promoting competition, complex financial arrangements including charges and exemptions, and covering the gaps left by the private market. In some cases, austerity measures actually increase the costs of the public sector: assessing cases individually, targeting, policing the boundaries and paying out for sub-contracted services end up costing more than the systems they replace.

Retrenchment, or cutting back, is a more accurate term than austerity: it is all about achieving reductions in costs and reductions in expenditure. Despite appearances, there has been less retrenchment than some of the rhetoric might seem to imply. European welfare states have done what they are meant to do: they have protected the economy from depression and severe shocks.[23] Similarly, the COVID-19 pandemic led to many countries adopting temporary measures to extend social provision. In the aftermath there has been a trend to trim back. Ortiz and Cummins, experts on issues relating to social protection, chart the implications for 172 countries. The cuts have been extensive. 120 countries have aimed to 'target' social protection, generally implying the introduction of tests and assessments to limit who can receive benefits. 91 have aimed to cut the wage bill for the public sector, 79 to extend privatization, 74 to trim back pensions.[24] But what is striking about this account is how strongly embedded the social provision is. Countries have not been abandoning their programmes. They have not been resetting things to where they were before.

Nearly 25 years ago, I wrote a book arguing that more states were taking on more responsibilities, and that this trend was growing. At the time, I thought this would be a long, slow process; I failed to recognize that the dam was about to burst. I would still hold, however, to another part of the same argument: that once a government has started to make provision, it is difficult politically for them to stop.[25] That effect is borne out by the experience of austerity. Attempts to cut back services are characterized by cheese-paring, trying to raise more money through tax and trying to shift responsibility into the private sector. They have not led to governments pulling out of the business of welfare altogether.

Conclusion: The future of welfare

The picture is messy. There is no uniform understanding of what makes a welfare state. There is enormous diversity of provision, and the services which are considered to be priorities are always subject to change. The rhetoric of universal citizenship is all too likely to be compromised by the practice of communitarianism. There is no common set of values, only a cacophony of competing aims and claims. And there is no consistency of approach – not in the principles applied by any particular country, and not even within the same services.

In general terms, the direction of movement has been leading towards the extension and expansion of social welfare services, but this has not been a smooth, consistent flow. There have been periods of inactivity and occasional retrenchment, interrupted by spells of brief, frenetic activity. The process of development calls for negotiation and adaptation, prompting the recognition of more extensive aims and objectives, as governments respond to claims made by their populations, compare themselves to their neighbours or simply bow to political pressures.

The issues considered in Chapter 7 may impair, and sometimes defeat, government priorities and intentions. There may be conflicting priorities in the policies of governments, who may be no less concerned with governance and legitimacy, economy and efficiency, and other policy priorities, such as economic development, securing partisan support and satisfying international organizations. And beyond policy, regardless of motivation and intention, the institutions and methods that are set up to realize the aspirations of policy have a logic and life of their own. There is always a gap between policy and implementation. Some part of this might be attributed to poor information, some part to the limited capacity of governments;[26] there may be obstacles set in the way, and so-called 'veto points' where some people – people elsewhere in government, other institutions or independent participants – can delay or block initiatives.[27]

Maybe the welfare state can be identified with a range of institutions, methods and services – that type of classification seems fairly arbitrary to me – but it is characterized no less by a set of principles and purposes. Those principles and purposes have the potential to be in conflict with each other, and disputes about the role and purpose of welfare states are inherent in the activity. The first of those conflicts lies between individualism and collectivism. Moral individualists see the freedom and dignity of the individual as paramount values; collectivists that those terms only acquire meaning in a social context, and that the duty of the state is to enhance the well-being of a society, not just of private individuals. Second, there is competition between neoliberals, who believe that private markets are the best way to commission and distribute goods and services, and social democrats, who think that government has to be guided by moral values, and that there is a moral duty to take responsibility for problems. Third, there is the divergence between universalism, and in particular universal human rights, and communitarianism. And fourth, there are the persistent dilemmas about who to include, who to serve and who not.

None of these conflicts is beyond resolution, or indeed of co-existence. The truth is that most people can sit quite comfortably while believing three or four apparently contradictory moral principles: they will try to strike a balance, rather than aiming for an absolute purity of purpose. This needs no apology.

NOTES

Chapter 1

1   W Trattner, 1974, *From Poor Law to welfare state*, New York: Free Press, p. 154; J Midgley, M Livermore, 2008, *The handbook of social policy*, Los Angeles: Sage, p. 367.

2   International Labour Organization, 2024, *World Social Protection Report 2024–26*, Geneva: International Labour Organization, p. xxiv.

3   World Bank/UNICEF, 2009, *Abolishing school fees in Africa*, Washington DC: World Bank, https://documents.worldbank.org/en/publication/documents-reports/documentdetail/780521468250868445/abolishing-school-fees-in-africa-lessons-from-ethiopia-ghana-kenya-malawi-and-mozambique

4   UNICEF, *State of the World's Children*, https://data.unicef.org/resources/dataset/the-state-of-the-worlds-children-2023-statistical-tables/, table 11.

5   International Labour Organization, 2024, ch. 3.

6   L Leisering, K Weible, 2024, Constructing social rights for the poor, in S Biswas, C Sambo, S Pellissery (eds), *The politics of welfare in the Global South*, Oxford: Oxford University Press.

7   *The Economist*, 2022, Just keep us alive, 5 February, pp. 54–6.

8   International Labour Organization, 2024, p. xx.

9   W Robson, 1976, *Welfare state and welfare society*, London: Allen & Unwin, p. 31.

10 F Nullmeier, F-X Kaufmann, 2021, Post war welfare state development, in D Béland, K Morgan, H Obinger, C Pierson (eds), *The Oxford handbook of the welfare state*, Oxford: Oxford University Press, p. 99.

11 D Garland, 2016, *The welfare state*, Oxford: Oxford University Press, p. 133.

12 J Kendall, M Knapp, 1994, A loose and baggy monster: boundaries, definitions and typologies, in J Smith, C Rochester, R Hedley, (eds), *Introduction to the voluntary sector*, London: Taylor & Francis.

13   D Beito, 1997, This enormous army: the mutual aid tradition of
     American fraternal societies before the twentieth century, *Social
     Philosophy and Policy*, 14(2), 20–38.

14   A Black, 1984, *Guilds and civil society in European political
     thought from the twelfth century to the present*, London:
     Routledge; J Brodman, 2009, *Charity and religion in medieval
     Europe*, Washington, DC: Catholic University of America Press.

15   J Veit-Wilson, 2000, States of welfare, *Social Policy and
     Administration*, 34(1), 1–25, p. 5, https://eprints.ncl.ac.uk/63239

16   City of Ypres, 1531, The government of poor relief (*Forma
     subventionis pauperum*), in P Spicker (ed), 2010, *The origins of
     modern welfare*, Bern: Peter Lang, https://rgu-repository.worktribe.
     com/OutputFile/1238885

17   G Esping-Andersen, 1990, *Three worlds of welfare capitalism*,
     Brighton: Polity.

18   F Castles, 2010, Black swans and elephants on the move, *Journal
     of European Social Policy*, 20(2), 92–101.

19   M Ferrera, 1996, The 'Southern Model' of welfare in social
     Europe, *Journal of European Social Policy*, 6(1), 17–37.

20   S Leibfried, 1991, *Towards a European welfare state?*, Bremen:
     Zentrum für Sozialpolitik.

21   C Aspalter (ed), 2020, *Ideal types in comparative social policy*,
     London: Routledge.

22   See C Bambra, 2007, Sifting the wheat from the chaff, *Social Policy
     and Administration*, 41(1), 1–28.

23   E Yörük, I Öker, G Tafoya, 2022, The four global worlds of
     welfare capitalism, *Journal of European Social Policy*, 32(2), 119–
     34; V Hasanaj, 2023, Global patterns of contemporary welfare
     states, *Journal of Social Policy*, 52(4), 886–922.

24   A Przeworski, H Teune, 1970, *The logic of comparative social
     inquiry*, New York: Wiley, p. 45.

25   K Leichsenring, 2020, Applying ideal types in long term care and
     analysis, in C Aspalter (ed), *Ideal types in comparative social
     policy*, London: Routledge.

26   D Garland, 2022, The emergence of the idea of the 'welfare state'
     in British political discourse, *History of the Human Sciences*, 35(1),
     132–57.

27   A Briggs, 1961, The welfare state in historical perspective,
     European Journal of Sociology, 2(2), 228–30.

28   R Titmuss, 1968, *Commitment to welfare*, London: Allen &
     Unwin, p. 129.

29   B Cantillon, 2022, *Poverty and the tragedy of the welfare state*, Antwerp: University of Antwerp, p. 4.

30   A Pollack, 2022, The proper role of the welfare state in a healthy capitalist system, *Michigan Journal of Economics*, https://sites.lsa. umich.edu/mje/2022/05/20/the-proper-role-of-the-welfare-state-in-a-healthy-capitalist-system/

31   Friedrich Ebert Stiftung, 2017, *The welfare state*, https://library.fes. de/pdf-files/iez/18542.pdf

32   R Sunak, 2024, Prime Minister's speech on welfare, https://www. gov.uk/government/speeches/prime-ministers-speech-on-welfare-19-april-2024

33   TH Marshall, 1963, *Sociology at the crossroads*, London: Heinemann, p. 87.

34   Esping-Andersen, 1990, p. 21.

Chapter 2

1   M Weber, 1918, Politics as a vocation, in HH Gerth, C Wright Mills, 1948, *From Max Weber*, London: RKP, pp. 77–8.

2   See, for example, the plans made by 67 governments at IMF, 2016, *Poverty reduction strategy papers*, https://www.imf.org/external/np/prsp/prsp.aspx

3   P Baldwin, 1990, *The politics of social solidarity*, Cambridge: Cambridge University Press; E Vriens, T De Moor, 2020, Mutuals on the move: exclusion processes in the welfare state and the rediscovery of mutualism, *Social Inclusion*, 8(1), 225–37.

4   G Cohn et al, 1894, cited in K Petersen, J Petersen, 2013, Confusion and divergence: origins and meanings of the term 'welfare state' in Germany and Britain, 1840–1940, *Journal of European Social Policy*, 23(1), 37–51.

5   E Burke, 1790, *Reflections on the revolution in France*, New York: Holt, Rinehart and Winston, 1959, p. 71.

6   A Vermuele, 2022, *Common good constitutionalism*, Cambridge: Polity Press.

7   A Smith, 1776, *The wealth of nations*, Book 5, ch. 1.

8   R Nozick, 1974, *Anarchy, state, and utopia*, New York: Basic Books.

9   JS Mill, 1848, *The principles of political economy*, Book 5, ch. 11.

10   N Ploug, J Kvist (eds), 1994, *Recent trends in cash benefits in Europe*, Copenhagen: Danish National Institute of Social Research.

11   For example, Swedish Social Democratic Party, 2007, *Our principles and values*, https://eprints.ncl.ac.uk/179576; Party of

European Socialists, 2011, *PES declaration of principles*, Brussels: PES.

12 K Marx, 1875, Critique of the Gotha programme.

13 C Attlee, 1945, Election address, *British Movietone News*, https://www.youtube.com/watch?v=Zlcn6JtQX_s

Chapter 3

1 For example, H Spencer, 1851, *Social statics*, New York: Schalkenbach Foundation, 1995.

2 For example, M Littlewood, 2012, The welfare state should be a safety net not a comfort blanket, https://www.dailymail.co.uk/debate/article-2090754/The-welfare-state-safety-net-comfort-blanket.html

3 R Titmuss, 1968, *Commitment to welfare*, London: Allen & Unwin.

4 C Murray, 1984, *Losing ground*, New York: Basic Books, pp. 16–17.

5 *Daily Telegraph*, 2015, The destructive effect of dependency on the state, 15 February, http://www.telegraph.co.uk/news/politics/conservative/11414430/The-destructive-effect-of-dependency-on-the-state.html

6 H Wilensky, C Lebeaux, 1958, *Industrial society and social welfare*, New York: Free Press, p. 147.

7 H Haber, 2020, The political economy of regulating for welfare: regulation preventing loss of access to basic services in the UK, Sweden, the EU, and Israel, *Annals of the American Academy of Political and Social Science*, 691(1), 50–67.

8 I Ortiz, 2007, *Social policy*, New York: United Nations Department for Economic and Social Affairs, http://esa.un.org/techcoop/documents/PN_SocialPolicyNote.pdf

9 R Chambers, 2007, *Poverty research: methodologies, mindsets and multidimensionality*, Brighton: Institute of Development Studies, p. 23.

10 International Labour Organization, n.d., *Social protection*, https://www.ilo.org/topics-and-sectors/social-protection

11 Asian Development Bank, 2003, *Social protection*, https://socialprotection.org/discover/publications/social-protection-our-framework-policies-and-strategies

12 L Doyal, I Gough, 1991, *A theory of human need*, London: Macmillan; M Nussbaum, 2006, Poverty and human functioning, in D Grusby, R Kanbur (eds), *Poverty and inequality*, Stanford: Stanford University Press.

13 A Sen, 1999, *Commodities and capabilities*, Oxford: Oxford University Press.
14 N Barr, 2004, *The economics of the welfare state*, Oxford: Oxford University Press.
15 L Feld, E Koehler, D Nientiedt, 2021, *Ordoliberalism and the social market economy*, Freiburg: University of Freiburg, http://hdl.handle.net/10419/232067
16 G Bramley, 1998, *Where does public spending go?*, London: Department of the Environment.
17 RH Tawney, 1931, *Equality*, London: Unwin, p. 122.
18 T Iversen, 2021, Democracy and capitalism, in D Béland, K Morgan, H Obinger, C Pierson (eds), *The Oxford handbook of the welfare state*, Oxford: Oxford University Press.
19 P Laroque, 1945, in M Lagrave, P Laroque, 2008, Hommage à Pierre Laroque à l'occasion du centenaire de sa naissance, *Revue française des affaires sociales*, 2008(1) 151–63.
20 R Lenoir, 1974, *Les exclus*, Paris: Seuil.
21 For example, S Stjernø, 2005, *Solidarity in Europe*, Cambridge: Cambridge University Press.
22 Pope John Paul II, 1987, *Sollicitudo rei socialis*, Vatican: Catholic Church, s. 38.
23 P Baldwin, 1990, *The politics of social solidarity*, Cambridge: Cambridge University Press, p. 33.
24 S Paugam, 2009, *La disqualification sociale*, Paris: Presses Universitaires de France.
25 KE Boulding, 1973, The boundaries of social policy, in WD Birrell, PAR Hillyard, AS Murie, DJD Roche (eds), *Social administration*, Penguin: Harmondsworth, p. 192.
26 Council of Europe, 2005, *Concerted development of social cohesion indicators: methodology guide*, Strasbourg: Council of Europe, pp. 24–6.
27 TH Marshall, 1950, *Citizenship and social class*, Cambridge: Cambridge University Press, p. 28.
28 R Lister, 1991, *The exclusive society*, London: Child Poverty Action Group.
29 H Dean, 2007, Social policy and human rights, *Social Policy and Society*, 7(1), 1–12.
30 Inter-American Court of Human Rights, 2003, Case of the 'Five Pensioners' v. Peru, Judgment of February 28, http://www.corteidh.or.cr/docs/casos/articulos/seriec_98_ing.pdf

31 G Esping-Andersen (ed), 2003, *Why we need a new welfare state*, Oxford: Oxford University Press.

32 A Hemerijck, 2017, *The uses of social investment*, Oxford: Oxford University Press.

33 I Plavgo, A Hemerijck, 2021, The social investment litmus test, *Journal of European Social Policy*, 31(3), 282–96.

34 B Cantillon, W van Lancker, 2013, Three shortcomings of the social investment perspective, *Social Policy and Society*, 12(4), 553–64.

35 J Stiglitz, 2017, *The welfare state in the twenty-first century*, New York: Roosevelt Institute.

36 R Bacon, W Eltis, 1978, *Britain's economic problem*, London: Macmillan.

37 M Mazzucato, 2015, *The entrepreneurial state*, New York: Anthem Press.

38 World Bank, 1994, *Adjustment in Africa: reforms, results and the road ahead*, Washington, DC: World Bank; D Dollar, J Svensson, 2000, What explains the success or failure of Structural Adjustment Programmes?, *Economic Journal*, 10, 894–917.

39 For example, Stiglitz, 2017; Ha-Joon Chang, 2011, *23 things they don't tell you about capitalism*, London: Penguin.

40 World Bank, 2013, *World Development Report 2013: Jobs*, Oxford: Oxford University Press, p. 21.

41 J Higgins, 1980, Social control theories of social policy, *Journal of Social Policy*, 9(1), 1–23.

42 *The Economist*, 2024, The pro-natalist turn, 25th May, pp. 67–9.

43 J Blakely, 2019, How economics becomes ideology, in P Róna, L Zsolnai (eds), *Agency and causal explanation in economics*, Cham: Springer.

44 C Murray, 1984, *Losing ground*, New York: Basic Books.

45 D Ameta, 2015, *Social protection and safety nets in Iran*, Brighton: Institute for Development Studies.

46 CA Crosland, 1956, *The future of socialism*, London: Jonathan Cape, p. 216.

Chapter 4

1 A Finkel, 2018, *Compassion*, London: Bloomsbury.

2 J Brodman, 2009, *Charity and religion in medieval Europe*, Washington, DC: Catholic University of America Press.

3 N Terpstra, 1994, Apprenticeship in social welfare, *Sixteenth Century Journal*, 25(1), 101–20.

4   A Gouldner, 1960, The norm of reciprocity, *American Sociological Review*, 25(2), 161–77.

5   R Titmuss, 1971, *The gift relationship*, Harmondsworth: Penguin.

6   M Sahlins, 1974, *Stone age economics*, London: Tavistock.

7   J Wolff, 2011, *Ethics and public policy*, Abingdon: Routledge, p. 82.

8   J-J Dupeyroux, 1989, *Droit de la securité sociale*, Paris: Dalloz, pp. 72n, 268n.

9   P Spicker, 2013, *Reclaiming individualism*, Bristol: Policy Press.

10 P Spicker, 2019, *Thinking collectively*, Bristol: Policy Press.

11 M Mazzucato, 2018, *The value of everything*, London: Penguin, ch. 3.

12 E Fukumoto, B Bozeman, 2019, Public values theory: what is missing?, *American Review of Public Administration*, 49(6), 635–48.

13 C Pierson, 2006, *Beyond the welfare state?*, Brighton: Polity.

14 F Eibl, 2020, *Social dictatorships*, Oxford: Oxford University Press.

15 T Dorlach, 2021, The causes of welfare state expansion in democratic middle-income countries, *Social Policy and Administration*, 55, 767–73.

16 A Sen, 2001, *Development as freedom*, Oxford: Oxford University Press.

17 J Habermas, 1976, *Legitimation crisis*, London: Heinemann.

18 A Vermuele, 2022, *Common good constitutionalism*, Cambridge: Polity Press.

19 R Nozick, 1974, *Anarchy, state, and utopia*, New York: Basic Books.

20 M Rothbard, 1978, *For a new liberty*, Auburn: von Mises Institute.

21 F Hayek, 1944, *The road to serfdom*, London: Routledge.

22 D Porteous ('A citizen of Glasgow'), 1783, *A letter to the citizens of Glasgow*, Glasgow: Robert Chapman, Alexander Duncan.

23 C Murray, 1984, *Losing ground*, New York: Basic Books.

24 S Christianson, 1993, Bad seed or bad science?, *New York Times*, 8 February.

25 P Lombardo, n.d., *Eugenic sterilization laws*, http://www.eugenicsarchive.org/html/eugenics/essay8text.html

26 E Carlson, 2001, *The unfit: a history of a bad idea*, New York: Cold Spring Harbor Laboratory Press.

27 R Macdonald, T Shildrick, A Furlong, 2013, In search of 'intergenerational cultures of worklessness': hunting the Yeti and shooting zombies, *Critical Social Policy*, 34(2), 199–220.

28   P Buhr, S Leibfried, 1995, What a difference a day makes, in G
      Room (ed), *Beyond the threshold*, Bristol: Policy Press; L Leisering,
      R Walker (eds), 1998, *The dynamics of modern society*, Bristol:
      Policy Press.

29   A Atkinson, A Maynard, C Trinder, 1983, *Parents and children*,
      London: Heinemann; I Kolvin, F Miller, D Scott, S Gatzanis,
      M Fleeting, 1990, *Continuities of deprivation?*, Aldershot: Avebury.

30   A Atkinson, 1995, *Incomes and the welfare state*, Cambridge:
      Cambridge University Press, ch. 6; Ha-Joon Chang, 2011, *23 things
      they don't tell you about capitalism*, London: Penguin, pp. 221ff.

Chapter 5

1   City of Ypres, 1531, The government of poor relief (*Forma
      subventionis pauperum*), in P Spicker (ed), 2010, *The
      origins of modern welfare*, Bern: Peter Lang, pp. 127–8,
      https://rgu-repository.worktribe.com/OutputFile/1238885

2   F Williams, 1992, Somewhere over the rainbow: universality and
      diversity in social policy, in N Manning, R Page (eds), *Social Policy
      Review 4*, Bristol: Social Policy Association, pp. 206–7.

3   M Walzer, 1983, *Spheres of justice*, New York: Basic Books, p. 9.

4   UN Declaration of the Rights of the Child, 1959, Principle 6.

5   S Edwards, 2005, *Disability: definitions, value and identity*,
      Abingdon: Radcliffe.

6   A Sen, 1999, *Commodities and capabilities*, Oxford: Oxford
      University Press.

7   M Ravallion, 2016, *The economics of poverty*, Oxford: Oxford
      University Press.

8   P Townsend, 1979, *Poverty in the United Kingdom*,
      Harmondsworth: Penguin, p. 36.

9   Sen, 1999.

10   D Narayan, R Chambers, M Shah, P Petesch, 2000, *Voices of the
      poor: crying out for change*, Washington, DC: World Bank/Oxford
      University Press.

11   See P Spicker, 2020, *The poverty of nations*, Bristol: Policy Press.

12   D Rasmussen, 1990, *Universalism versus communitarianism*,
      Cambridge, MA: MIT Press.

13   J Seekings, 2024, Conditional and unconditional universalism, in
      S Biswas, C Sambo, S Pellissery (eds), *The politics of welfare in the
      Global South*, Oxford: Oxford University Press.

14   Council of Europe, 2005, *Concerted development of social cohesion
      indicators: methodology guide*, Strasbourg: Council of Europe.

15 For example, L Bourgeois, 1896, *Solidarisme*, Paris: Armand Colin; M Mauss, 1924, *Essai sur le don*, http://classiques.uqac.ca/classiques/mauss_marcel/socio_et_anthropo/2_essai_sur_le_don/essai_sur_le_don.pdf

16 P Jones, 1990, Universal principles and particular claims, in A Ware, RE Goodin (eds), *Needs and welfare*, London: Sage, p. 40.

Chapter 6

1 A Smith, 1776, *The wealth of nations*, Book 1, ch. 2.

2 M Blaug, 2007, The fundamental theorems of welfare economics, historically contemplated, *History of Political Economy*, 39(2), 185–207.

3 P Spicker, 2013, *Reclaiming individualism*, Bristol: Policy Press, pp. 89–97.

4 R Wilkinson, K Pickett, 2009, *The spirit level*, London: Allen Lane.

5 A Ryan, 1989, Value judgements and welfare, in D Helm (ed), *The economic borders of the state*, Oxford: Oxford University Press,

6 R Starr, 2011, *General equilibrium theory*, Cambridge: Cambridge University Press, pp. 213–14.

7 J Barlow, S Duncan, 1994, *Success and failure in housing provision*, Oxford: Pergamon, ch. 1.

8 UN Habitat, 2016, *Slum Almanac 2015–2016*, Nairobi: UN-Habitat, pp. 2, 4.

9 J Stiglitz, 2017, *The welfare state in the twenty-first century*, New York: Roosevelt Institute.

10 For example, M Friedman, 1962, *Capitalism and freedom*, Chicago: University of Chicago Press.

11 M Friedman, 1953, The methodology of positive economics, in *Essays in positive economics*, Chicago: University of Chicago Press; and see P Spicker, 2016, Economics as practical wisdom, *Real World Economics Review*, 75, 113–25.

12 D Graeber, 2014, *Debt*, Brooklyn: Melville House Publishing.

13 S Ison, S Wall, 2007, *Economics*, Harlow: Prentice-Hall.

14 E Vriens, T De Moor, 2020, Mutuals on the move: exclusion processes in the welfare state and the rediscovery of mutualism, *Social Inclusion*, 8(1), 225–37.

15 M Mazzucato, 2015, *The entrepreneurial state*, New York: Anthem Press.

16 J Le Grand, 1992, The theory of government failure, *British Journal of Political Science*, 21(4), 423–42.

17 G Tullock, 2002, The theory of public choice, in G Tullock, A Seldon, G Brady (eds), *Government failure*, Washington, DC: Cato Institute.

Chapter 7

1 World Bank, 1993, *World Development Report 1993: Investing in Health*, Oxford: Oxford University Press, https://documents. worldbank.org/en/publication/documents-reports/documentdetail/ 468831468340807129/world-development-report-1993-investing-in-health

2 See BMJ Global Health 2023, *Country experiences of developing UHC packages*, vol 8, supplement 1.

3 Australian Aid, 2011, *Targeting the poorest*, https://www.dfat. gov.au/about-us/publications/Pages/targeting-the-poorest-an-assessment-of-the-proxy-means-test-methodology

4 E Dadap-Cantal, A Fischer, C Ramos, 2021, Targeting versus social protection in cash transfers in the Philippines, *Critical Social Policy*, 41(3), 364–84.

5 S Kidd, G Nycander, A Tran, M Cretney, 2020, *The social contract and the role of universal social security in building trust in government*, Uppsala: Church of Sweden/Development Pathways, p. 18.

6 S Osborne, Z Radnor, G Nasi, 2013, A new theory for public service management?, *American Review of Public Administration*, 43(2), 135–58.

7 F Juuko, C Kabonesa, 2007, *Universal primary education in contemporary Uganda*, Kampala: Makarere University Human Rights and Peace Centre, https://www.yumpu.com/en/document/ view/6721728/universal-primary-education-upe-in-contemporary-uganda

8 World Bank/UNICEF, 2009, *Abolishing school fees in Africa*, Washington, DC: World Bank, https://documents.worldbank.org/ en/publication/documents-reports/documentdetail/ 780521468250868445/abolishing-school-fees-in-africa-lessons-from-ethiopia-ghana-kenya-malawi-and-mozambique

9 K Lindert, T Karippacheril, I Rodríguez Caillava, K Chávez, 2020, *Sourcebook on the foundations of social protection delivery systems*, Washington, DC: World Bank.

10 See A Downes, S Lansley, eds, 2018, *It's basic income*, Bristol: Policy Press.

11 P Spicker, 2019, Some reservations about basic income, in
    M Danson, C Goodman, J Perry (eds), *Exploring basic income in
    Scotland*, Glasgow: Scottish Universities Insight Unit.

12 R Titmuss, 1968, Universal and selective social services, in
    Commitment to welfare, London: Allen & Unwin.

13 M Mazzucato, 2018, *The value of everything*, London: Penguin,
    ch. 3.

14 D Garland, 2016, *The welfare state*, Oxford: Oxford University
    Press, pp. 82–3.

15 P Baldwin, 1990, *The politics of social solidarity*, Cambridge:
    Cambridge University Press.

16 B Obama, 2010, Remarks by the President at Laborfest in
    Milwaukee, Wisconsin, https://obamawhitehouse.archives.gov/
    the-press-office/2010/09/06/remarks-president-laborfest-milwaukee-
    wisconsin

17 See OECD at https://data.oecd.org/emp/labour-force-participation-
    rate.htm

18 Ha-Joon Chang, 2011, *23 things they don't tell you about
    capitalism*, London: Penguin, pp. 228–30.

19 A Hemerijck, M Matsaganis, 2024, *Who's afraid of the welfare
    state now?*, Oxford: Oxford University Press, p. 278.

Chapter 8

1   S Leibfried, 1991, *Towards a European welfare state?*, Bremen:
    Zentrum für Sozialpolitik.

2   C Offe, 1984, *Contradictions of the welfare state*, London:
    Hutchison, p. 153.

3   H Wilensky, C Lebeaux, 1958, *Industrial society and social
    welfare*, New York: Free Press.

4   R Titmuss, 1974, *Social policy*, London: Allen & Unwin.

5   G Esping-Andersen, 1990, *Three worlds of welfare capitalism*,
    Brighton: Polity.

6   S Ringen, 1989, *The possibility of politics*, Oxford: Clarendon
    Press; R Mishra, 1990, *The welfare state in capitalist society*, New
    York: Harvester Wheatsheaf.

7   Swedish Social Democratic Party, 2007, *Our principles and values*,
    https://eprints.ncl.ac.uk/179576

8   I Gough, F Wood, 2004, *Insecurity and welfare regimes in Asia,
    Africa and Latin America*, Cambridge: Cambridge University Press.

9   R Mishra, 1981, *Society and social policy*, London: Macmillan.

10 Esping-Andersen, 1990.

11   L Leisering, 2018, *The global rise of social cash transfers*, Oxford: Oxford University Press; L Leisering (ed), 2021, *One hundred years of social protection*, Cham: Palgrave Macmillan.

12   M Sahlins, 1974, *Stone age economics*, London: Tavistock.

13   K Celestino, 2023, The clandestine welfare: the role of illicit actors in the provision of social protection in Latin America, *Journal of International and Comparative Social Policy*, doi:10.1017/ics.2023.10

14   United Nations, 1948, *Universal Declaration of Human Rights*, Article 22.

15   A Sen, 1999, *Development as freedom*, Oxford: Oxford University Press.

16   S Radelet, 2010, *Emerging Africa?*, Baltimore: Center for Global Development.

17   See, for example, D Niemann, D Krogmann, K Martens, 2022, Between economics and education: how international organizations changed the view on education, in F Nullmeier, D Gonzales de Reufels, H Obinger (eds), *International impacts on social policy*, London: Palgrave Macmillan.

18   International Monetary Fund, 2016, *Poverty Reduction Strategy Papers*, https://www.imf.org/external/np/prsp/prsp.aspx

19   K Birchler, S Limpach, K Michaelowa, 2016, Aid modalities matter, *International Studies Quarterly*, 60(3), 427–39.

20   UNICEF, 2023, *State of the World's Children: Statistical Tables*, table 2, https://www.unicef.org/reports/state-worlds-children-2023

21   For example, M Sissons, P French (eds), 1963, *The age of austerity 1945–51*, Harmondsworth: Penguin.

22   S Konzelmann, 2019, *Austerity*, Cambridge: Polity, p. 1.

23   A Hemerijck, M Matsaganis, 2024, *Who's afraid of the welfare state now?*, Oxford: Oxford University Press, pp. 268ff.

24   I Ortiz, M Cummins, 2022, *End austerity*, Action Aid International and eleven other publishers, https://www.cadtm.org/End-Austerity-A-Global-Report-on-Budget-Cuts-and-Harmful-Social-Reforms-in-2022

25   P Spicker, 2000, *The welfare state: a general theory*, London: Sage.

26   *The Economist*, 2022, Just keep us alive, 5 February, pp. 54–6.

27   J Pressman, A Wildavsky, 1992, *Implementation*, Berkeley: University of California Press.

FURTHER READING

P Baldwin, 1990, *The politics of social solidarity*, Cambridge: Cambridge University Press.

D Béland, R Mahon, 2016, *Advanced introduction to social policy*, Cheltenham: Edward Elgar.

S Biswas, C Sambo, S Pellissery (eds) 2024, *The politics of welfare in the Global South*, Oxford: Oxford University Press.

City of Ypres, 1531, The government of poor relief (*Forma subventionis pauperum*), in P Spicker (ed), 2010, *The origins of modern welfare*, Bern: Peter Lang, https://rgu-repository.worktribe.com/OutputFile/1238885

F Eibl, 2020, *Social dictatorships*, Oxford: Oxford University Press.

T Fitzpatrick, 2011, *Welfare theory*, London: Bloomsbury.

D Garland, 2016, *The welfare state*, Oxford: Oxford University Press.

L Gregory, 2018, *Exploring welfare debates*, Bristol: Policy Press.

International Labour Organization, 2023, *World Social Protection Report 2024–26*, Geneva: International Labour Organization.

L Leisering, 2018, *The global rise of social cash transfers*, Oxford: Oxford University Press.

L Leisering (ed), 2021, *One hundred years of social protection*, Cham: Palgrave Macmillan.

C Pierson, F Castles, I Neumann (eds), 2013, *The welfare state reader*, Brighton: Polity.

A Sen, 2001, *Development as freedom*, Oxford: Oxford University Press.

P Spicker, 2023, *States and welfare states*, Bristol: Policy Press.

United Nations Children's Fund, 2016, *The State of the World's Children: a fair chance for every child*, New York: United Nations Children's Fund; and see current statistics at https://data.unicef.org/resources/

United Nations Development Project, 2024, *Human Development Report 2023–24*, New York: United Nations Development Project.

J Veit-Wilson, 2000, States of welfare, *Social Policy and Administration*, 34(1), 1–25, https://eprints.ncl.ac.uk/63239

INDEX